PHOTOGRAPHING
CHILDREN

John Hedgecoe's
MASTER CLASSES IN PHOTOGRAPHY

PHOTOGRAPHING
CHILDREN

Galley Press

John Hedgecoe's Master Classes in Photography
PHOTOGRAPHING CHILDREN
was edited and designed by
Mitchell Beazley Publishers Limited

This edition published 1985 by Galley Press, an imprint
of W. H. Smith and Son Limited, Registered No. 237811
England. Trading as WHS Distributors, St. John's House,
East Street, Leicester LE1 6NE
ISBN 0 86136 769 3

Photoset in Great Britain by Tradespools Limited
Originated in Great Britain by Culver Graphics Litho Limited
Printed and bound in Hong Kong
by Mandarin Publishers Limited.

Contents

Introduction

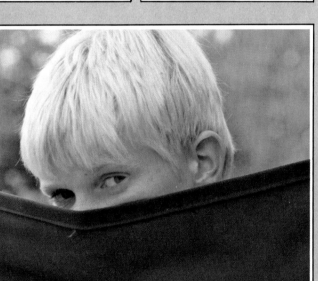

As subjects for photography, children are of universal and inexhaustible interest. Even when they are not our own, their spontaneity, energy and expressiveness make them subjects of unequalled appeal in many branches of photography, whether it is candid or studio work, portraiture or photojournalism.

In planning the first of the Master Classes, I wanted the approach to the "how" and "why" of photographing children to combine teaching and demonstration from every helpful viewpoint. There are, therefore, five strands in which I cover every aspect of child photography. I begin with a short portfolio, in which I have aimed to convey my own fascination with and enjoyment in this field of photography. The following section, on appropriate cameras and equipment, puts in perspective the vast choice now available to amateurs and professionals.

In the first of the two principal sections of the book, Applying the photographer's skills, I deal with the basic elements of photography, such as handling shutter speed or depth of field, in the light of the special requirements of child photography. The teaching steps are backed up with photographs in colour demonstrating the way I have applied the relevant skills in my own work.

The second main section, Analysing the photographer's craft, takes as its theme a Photodiary covering the development of children from birth to adolescence. The photographs in colour on this theme are supported by an analysis of the factors — sometimes compositional, sometimes technical — that I have borne in mind to achieve the results I wanted.

I have concluded my Master Class with a Photofeature which, I hope, will be an inspiration to students and aspiring professionals looking for projects of commercial value.

Pentax, 100 mm, 1/125, f4,
Kodachrome 64.
Dreams and reflections

Pentax, 50 mm, 1/1000, f16,
Ektachrome 200.
Making the big splash

Leicaflex, 135 mm, 1/500,
Ektachrome 400.
The party is over.

Pentax, 135 mm, 1/125, f8,
Kodachrome 64.
A decision of importance

Contax, 35 mm, 1/125, f8,
Ektachrome 64.
A sense for the order in things

Pentax, 100 mm, 1/60, f2.8,
Kodachrome 64.
Silhouetted figure in a circle

Pentax, 100 mm, 1/60, f2.8,
Kodachrome 64.
Gymnast—just holding on

Pentax, 100 mm, 1/30, f16,
Ektachrome 160 tungsten.
The observer observed

Choosing a camera

Of the many types of cameras available, the best all-round camera is the 35 mm single-lens reflex (SLR). Models available range from reasonably priced cameras with simple controls to expensive and highly sophisticated pieces of equipment, offering facilities which the beginner may not initially feel the need to use.

An SLR has many advantages. It enables you to maintain full control over focusing, aperture and shutter speed. Through the viewfinder you see exactly what the film will register when you actually take the picture. Light entering the lens is diverted to the viewfinder by a system of mirror and prism. Thus, when you vary the focusing and framing of the image you can watch it change in the viewfinder. Likewise, the depth of field can be seen and controlled.

Many SLR cameras have built-in light metering—sometimes known as through-the-lens metering (TTL). Advances in technology are largely directed at the SLR because of its deserved popularity, ensuring that it becomes increasingly sophisticated and remains competitively priced. It is also easy to handle and use—significant advantages under any circumstances but particularly so when fast-moving children are the chosen subjects.

Although supplied with a standard (50 or 55 mm) lens that is ideal for general photography, the SLR will accept a large variety of lenses and accessories, enabling you to build up a system of greater capacity. There are occasions when a standard lens can lead to frustration because the photographer cannot get close enough to capture interesting detail on a subject (for example, a child running about in the middle of a football pitch), or cannot get far enough away to include the whole scene (a view of the entire game). The addition of appropriate lenses—in this case a telephoto lens and a wide-angle lens—to your system will allow you to overcome most of these problems. SLR has opened up the possibility of a total sy —a single camera body which can be fitted the appropriate attachments for photograp subjects as different as the moon and microsc life.

There is a great variety of 35 mm film, desi to help the photographer operate success under the widest range of conditions. Film 35 mm, whether used in an SLR or another of camera, has another virtue. The mode negative size (24 × 36 mm) means that 36 or n exposures per roll can be provided. The car does not need to be reloaded as frequently as ot and wastage is not a major concern, encoura, the urge to experiment. This is the best wa improving camera skills and ability.

Larger rollfilm SLR cameras can also form basis of highly advanced systems. The stan negative size is 6 cm ($2\frac{1}{4}$ in) square, four ti

Simple instant picture cameras, like the Polaroid 1000 (left), have direct vision viewfinders, focus down to 0.75 m ($2\frac{1}{2}$ ft) and have integral light meters giving automatic exposure over a limited range of stops and shutter speeds.

The simplest 110 camera of the kind shown above has elementary focusing and exposure controls. Many basic 110s have built-in electronic flash and another lens (tele or close-up), which is easily slid into place.

An advanced camera like the Pentax SLR (below) has through the-lens metering and accepts interchangeable lenses, making it capable of high quality work in a wide variety of conditions.

Advanced Polaroid Sonar Autofocus cameras have automatic exposure controls over a good range of stops and shutter speeds, and offer automatic focusing. Can produce quality work.

Most instant cameras now use dry-process film, where the negative is processed and a print produced within one piece of material— a white plastic card, which is ejected from the camera after each exposure. The image appears on one side, slowly reaching full density. It is then permanent. The maximum print size is 108 × 89 mm ($4\frac{1}{4}$ × $3\frac{1}{2}$ in).

Easy-to-load cartrid film for 110 cameras has a negative size o 13 × 17 mm. This is i small to produce lar, blow-up prints, thou it produces quite sat factory results up to postcard size. If 110 colour transparenci are taken, they shou be viewed on a spec 110 projector, thoug it is possible to use a standard 35 mm projector.

er than a 35 mm negative. Although a 35 mm native can be enlarged to a great size, it must be igh technical quality to produce a good result. re comes a point where the larger negative always give better image quality. Some 6 cm (2¼ in sq) SLR cameras offer the real antage of an interchangeable back, which ws a different film to be used for alternate ts. These cameras are expensive in comparison h the 35 mm SLR and not so convenient to use. A simpler 6 × 6 cm (2¼ in sq) camera is the R (twin-lens reflex). This has two lenses of tical focal length, one for viewing and one for ning the image on film. Focusing is con-ient—the image which appears on the view-ler screen is the same size as that which appears the negative, but reversed left to right. TLR eras permit the image to be seen through the wfinder during the actual exposure. On an R camera the mirror flips up when the shutter

is pressed to allow light to reach the film, and so the viewfinder is closed off and the image momen-tarily cannot be seen. On the other hand, the TLR is bulky and few models can accept interchange-able lenses. It is also subject to parallax error, because there is a slight difference in viewpoint between the top (viewing) lens and the lower (taking) lens, and this is noticeable in close-up work. Some TLR cameras have a parallax correction device built into the focusing screen.

There are plenty of compact, inexpensive direct vision 35 mm cameras on the market. They are generally equipped with simple controls—often with fully automatic light metering—which make them very easy to operate. They give a sharp, bright view of the subject and can be used without constant adjustment. Advanced direct vision cameras offer a rangefinder facility to ensure accurate focusing. Two images appear in the view-finder. The focusing ring is turned until they

coincide, and the camera is then perfectly focused. Some will take interchangeable lenses.

The 110 pocket camera is small enough to carry in a pocket or handbag and simple to use. In the most basic models there is no means of varying exposure or focusing; others are more versatile, having interchangeable lenses and automatically controlled exposure. Generally, though, the small negative size makes it hard to obtain good quality prints larger than 10 × 12.5 cm (4 × 5 in).

Instant cameras issue a finished, permanent print within seconds of exposure. The film is ex-pensive but there are no processing costs, unless additional prints are required. The more expensive instant cameras incorporate focusing and aperture controls, allowing excellent results to be obtained even under difficult conditions. Professional pho-tographers often use an advanced instant camera to check exposure before shooting a particular subject.

The non-reflex 35 mm camera (left) has an accurate rangefinder linked to the focusing ring. This is linked to the lens and shutter allowing manual adjustment of the aperture and shutter speed. The lens is not interchangeable.

The basic 6 × 6 cm (2¼ in sq) camera is the TLR (left) with an upper lens for viewing and lower for exposing. The more complex SLR type (below) accepts a full range of lenses and accessories. The fold-ing hoods shade the viewfinder screens from extraneous light reflection.

Typical 35 mm SLR (right) will have auto/manual exposure con-trol by TTL metering; shutter speeds that range from a second to 1/1000; a standard lens opening to f1.2, f1.4, f1.8 or f2 and will accept a variety of alternative lenses.

Cassettes for 35 mm film contain 20, 24 or 36 exposure lengths. The narrow leader strip is threaded into a slit in the camera's take-up spool and the perfora-tions on both edges of the film engage on toothed sprockets which advance the film when the winder is operated. The film must always be wound back into the cassette after use.

Rollfilm for cameras taking 6 × 6 cm (2¼ in sq) format is paper-backed in 12- or 24-exposure lengths and the variety available is comparable to the 35 mm film range. It is loaded by threading a paper leader into a slot on the take-up spool. After full exposure, the film is sealed with gummed paper to prevent accidental fogging.

The controls of a camera

rewind knob

viewfinder window

film cassette

lens

iris diaphragm

This simple camera illustrates the basic principle of all photography. Light passes through a lens and strikes light-sensitive film, which reacts to the amount of light reaching it and records the image. If the film is to be exposed correctly, the amount of light passing through the lens must be exactly controlled.

When photographing children, it is often desirab to capture fleeting moments before they are lo Being prepared is not a problem with simp cameras, where you load the film and are ready shoot, and the many sophisticated automa cameras now on the market. However, ma excellent cameras are operated manually, requing setting before taking an exposure. Ma automatic cameras have override facilities f manual operation.

Familiarity with the controls ensures that time is wasted when shooting. Set the camera prevailing conditions. Adjustments may be need from time to time, but making these should r result in missing the picture. The relationship children to the activity that they are involved

Focusing on simple cameras may be fixed or limited to a number of fixed ranges. The SLR is focused by twisting a ring on the lens barrel. It is designed to be large enough to be manipulated easily while looking through the viewfinder. When the subject is sharp, the camera is focused correctly. SLRs are also fitted with a device which aids focusing by fragmenting an area in the centre of the viewfinder when the lens is out of focus—useful for close-range work, where there is less room for error. Viewing is best carried out at full aperture for maximum clarity of view. The aperture is then stopped down prior to exposure. On many SLRs this function is automatic. The depth of field is the zone of acceptable sharpness extending in front of and behind the point of sharpest focus.

Most SLR cameras have the shutter speed contro on top of the body, as shown left. The ASA setting is often incorporated into the shutter speed control. Many cameras have a "B" setting at whit the shutter remains open for as long as the butto is depressed, for time exposures. The "X" or arro symbol provides synchronization for electronic flash. The bulb symbol shows the speed to use fo bulb flash. The slowest shutter speed at which a non-professional can hand-hold a camera is 1/30 at slower speeds a tripod must be used to elimina camera-shake, preferably in conjunction with a cable release to overcome the camera shake caused by pressing the release button. Even at speeds of 1/60 and 1/30, a firm grip and stance are essential to avoid movement.

Selective focusing can produce varying pictures from a similar viewpoint, allowing alternative emphasis to be placed on the same scene. Opening up the aperture reduces the depth of field and enables you to focus selectively. I took both photographs of the girls playing cricket at f2. In the top one I concentrated on the girl with the bat, picking a moment of maximum activity as the bat was lifted and her foot moved forward, her face showing fierce determination. The position of the ball reinforces the stress. The bowler's presence and contribution is recorded but not stressed. In the lower photograph the emphasis is reversed. Here the bowler, complete with ball, is the focus of attention and the girl with the bat becomes a passive element of the composition.

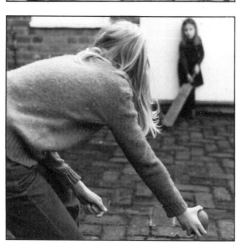

Movement can be communicated in different ways. In the upper photograph I set the shutter speed at 1/60. This was too slow to arrest the movement of the girl on the bicycle and consequently the image contains no detail. But the blurred effect heightens the feeling of speed while leaving the nature of the activity clear. You may choose to achieve an entirely different way of recording the same activity, as I did on the girl's return journey, selecting a shutter speed of 1/250 to freeze all movement. The result is this sharply-detailed composition with a pyramid effect. The sense of movement is communicated by the angle of the bicycle and by the whole pose—head down, muscles straining to propel the machine forward.

resultant expressions, movements and atti-
must all be recorded in split seconds and
photographs should not be sacrificed in a
minute attempt to adjust the controls more
sely.

rst choose your film. The ASA, DIN or ISO
ber indicates the film speed—the higher the
ber, the faster the film. Adjust the film speed
ator on the camera to the appropriate figure.
exposure indicated by the meter will be
rned by the film speed setting.

he camera has three main controls: aperture,
er speed and focus. The aperture (f-stop) de-
ines the amount of light let in by the iris or
ragm. The shutter speed dictates how long
lm is exposed to that light. Focus affects the

degree of sharpness or blurring of objects in the
photograph. Aperture and focus controls take the
form of rotating rings set into the lens barrel;
the shutter speed setting may also be on the lens
mount but more usually on the camera body itself.

Most speed settings are marked in fractions of a
second, from one second to 1/1000, with each pro-
gressive setting being twice as fast as the previous
one. Aperture settings also follow a standard geo-
metric scale from f1.2 to f22, and beyond; each increase of f-number halves the amount of light
passing through the lens. The widest aperture (the
one letting in most light) of a standard 50 mm may
be f1.2, f1.8, f2 or f2.8 depending on make.

Correct exposure may be achieved through
various combinations of aperture and speed set-

ting: the faster the speed, the larger the aperture
needed to let in the same amount of light, and vice
versa. The two scales are directly related. If light
conditions call for an exposure of 1/125 at f11, but
a speed of twice that is needed to freeze a child in
motion, constant exposure may be maintained by
setting the speed to 1/250 and doubling the aperture to f8. Speed is doubled and so is aperture size.

To set the camera in preparation for a photographic session, set the shutter speed first—1/125 is
suitable for stationary subjects, 1/250 if the subject
is moving. Then take a light reading to establish
the appropriate f-stop setting. Providing there is
adequate light (if not, you will have to reduce the
shutter speed) and you have selected a fast enough
film, you can now focus and begin to shoot.

The aperture setting is closely related to depth of
field, which is the distance at which a three-
dimensional subject can be brought into
acceptably sharp focus. If you focus on a child in
the middle distance, and a house in the background is also in focus, the picture will have great
depth of field. Most sophisticated cameras provide
a depth-of-field scale on the lens barrel which
relates depth of field, aperture setting and
distance of subject. Some SLRs enable the depth
of field to be studied in the viewfinder at the touch
of a button. The depth of field increases with
distance between camera and subject. As a
general rule, greater depth of field can be
achieved by stopping down the aperture and
decreasing shutter speed.

Built-in electronic flash (left) is not a standard
camera control, but it is increasingly available on
sophisticated 110 and 35 mm viewfinder cameras,
opening up new photographic possibilities indoors
and out. Electronic flash is largely superseding
bulb flash—it casts better light and gives a large
number of flashes before the batteries run down.
Such units may have rechargeable batteries for
use with a mains adaptor. However, built-in fixed
flash has certain disadvantages. There is no way of
"bouncing" the light to the subject, which
eliminates harsh shadows, and the range and
power of built-in flash rarely compares with that
of detachable flash units. In colour photographs, if
subjects show red eyes it is because the flash has
been too close to the lens-subject line.

two cricketers
g by the tree show
the depth of field is
ed by adjusting the
ture setting. The
picture, which I
with the aperture
open, has a
w depth of field
he result is that
the girl in the
ground is in sharp
s. By stopping
n to f16, however,
adjusting the
ter speed so that
ame amount of
is registered on
lm, I recorded a
h greater depth
ld. The whole
ure area, the back-
nd as well as the
, is in sharp focus,
all details show up
ly in the
ograph.

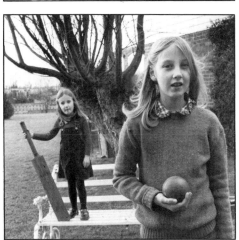

Automatic or meter-
equipped cameras
calculate exposure by
averaging readings
from highlight and
shadow. This works
well shooting with the
light or in overcast
conditions but, when
faced with very bright
highlights or shooting
against strong light,
underexposure will
result. Some automatic
cameras have a manual
override to allow you to
adjust for these con-
ditions. In these two
pictures, the girl was
standing against a
bright sky, the sun
behind her. In the top
photograph, exposed
for the highlights, she
has become completely
silhouetted. If I had
taken a reading from
her face alone, the sky
would have bleached
out entirely. To fill in
details of her face and
keep the strong cloud
shapes, I used daylight
flash—on an automatic
camera without manual
override this would
have been the only
option open to me.

Light meters and flash equipment

Correct exposure is fundamental to photography. Unless you have a camera with fixed controls, some kind of light metering is essential. Advances in camera technology have resulted in increasing availability of cameras with built-in metering systems so that hand-held meters are now used mainly for specialized purposes.

Built-in metering comes in various forms. The simplest is a meter situated on the top of the camera which indicates the required aperture setting and shutter speed, which must then be set manually. In semi-automatic cameras the meter is coupled to exposure controls. The photographer sets either aperture or shutter speed and the other is set automatically. Alternatively, one control is set and a needle visible in the viewfinder moves as the other control is altered. When the needle is centred, the camera is correctly set. Fully automatic cameras calculate correct exposure and set the controls ready for use. In advanced cameras the chosen settings are displayed in the viewfinder. An override system allows the automatic camera to be set manually when required.

Some cameras—like the pocket-sized 110 shown here—are fully automatic. Exposure is calculated and controls set automatically, but there is no manual override. The SLR (left) is semi-automatic with through-the-lens metering. One control, in this case the shutter, is pre-set while the other, the diaphragm ring, is turned by hand until the needle in the viewfinder is centred in the circular mark indicating the correct exposure setting.

A quality hand-held exposure meter is often used by photographers who want maximum accuracy and it gives two types of reading. A reflected reading records the amount of light reflecting back from the subject. An incident light reading measures light falling on the subject. It is taken by sliding a diffuser cone over the cell, which is then pointed back at the light source. Incident readings are difficult with built-in meters.

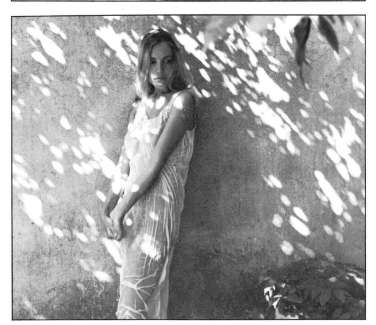

Great care must be taken when shooting certain kinds of subject —especially with built-in meters. If a subject contains strong highlights and shadows, problems will be caused by the meter's response to the intense highlights. Meters cannot balance both extremes and come up with a correct median reading. In order to ensure that shadow and highlight are both properly represented when one outweighs the other, it is necessary to take two readings, one of the darkest significant shadow and one of the brightest significant highlight. If the two are averaged and the camera set accordingly, the result will be a more accurate reflection of the picture's tonal extremes. In the top photograph of the girl, the exposure was set for the brightest part of this high-contrast composition. As a result, a rather gloomy feel was created, with loss of detail in shadow areas. In the centre photograph, the opposite effect was achieved by using a shadow reading, with consequent overexposure elsewhere. The bottom picture is the best, showing the combination of light and shadow that made the composition so effective. It was the result of a setting mid-way between highlight and shadow readings. Care must be taken when a subject is being taken against the light if detailing is required. If flash or a reflector are not available to light the shadow areas and it is imperative that you shoot from that direction, expose for the shadow area only.

use of additional artificial light extends the
[ran]ge of photographic possibilities. The most
[basic] form is bulb flash, either in the form of single
[bulbs] (used in a special holder) or the more modern
[flash]cubes that fit directly onto the camera. Bulb
[flash] is expensive because bulbs or cubes are dis-
[card]ed after one use.

[E]lectronic flash gives repeated use from the
[sam]e tube. Although initially more expensive than
[bulb] flash, it is better value in the long term. It
[com]es in various forms, from a unit that is fitted
[to t]he camera to large studio units used away from
[the c]amera. An alternative is tungsten studio light-
[ing] which has the advantages of low cost and the
[light]ing effect can be fully observed before
[expo]sing.

[F]lash, on the other hand, has a particular virtue
[whe]n photographing children. Their quick and
[ofte]n unexpected movements can spoil a picture,
[unle]ss the camera is set at a high shutter speed.
[The] high speed of the flash itself—between 1/750
[and] 1/2000 depending on make and size—acts as a
[shut]ter and arrests all movement.

Electronic flash comes
in many forms. It may
be built into a camera
(top left) or detachable,
as with the 110 (centre
left). A more powerful
and versatile electronic
unit (bottom left) pre-
vents harsh shadows
by bouncing light off its
own reflector card. The
tungsten lamp (centre)
is a typical studio lamp
with a large reflector,
giving soft, diffused
light from a frosted
bulb. To produce light
of a similar quality, its
electronic counterpart
points into an umbrella
reflector.

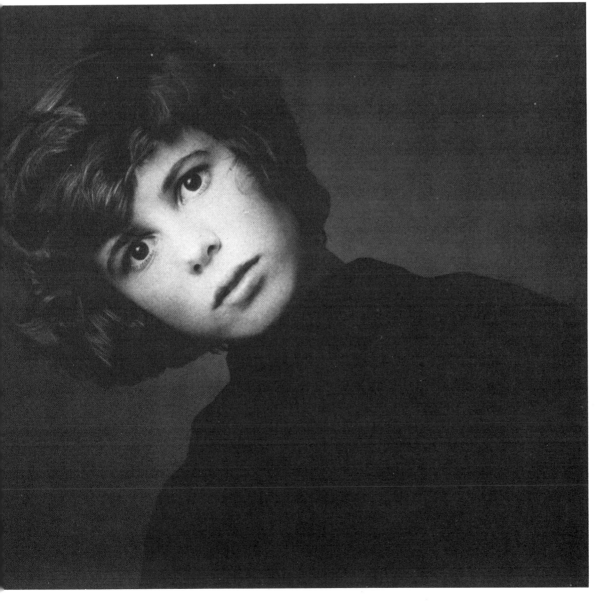

An eerie effect with
the face highlighted
dramatically was
achieved by using a
spotlight fitted with a
conical snoot to direct
the light beam onto a
restricted area of the
child's face. A similar
effect could be
achieved with an
ordinary domestic
reading lamp with a
cone made of white
card. I exposed for the
highlights, resulting in
a burning-out of detail
in the face and the loss
of almost all back-
ground detail. The
dark clothing helps
this effect.

Studio equipment

The photographer's workshop is the studio, designed to give complete control over lighting conditions and background for indoor photography. A studio can be anything from an empty room with white walls, natural light, camera and reflector to a complex place packed with sophisticated equipment. It is possible to create a simple studio at home, provided certain requirements can be met, which will increase opportunities for developing new skills and undertaking a variety of work.

There must be a good source of natural light (which can be closed off with blinds or shutters, permitting the use of artificial light during the day) and sufficient working space. A minimum of two metres (six feet) is required for background and backlighting behind the subject, and a similar distance between camera and subject. The shortest workable length of a studio is therefore four metres (twelve feet) though six metres (twenty feet) is ideal.

Walls and ceilings should be white, though one black or dark grey wall can be useful. Matt paint prevents unwanted reflection. The floor should be easy to clean to prevent a build-up of dust. If there is no suitable spare room, consider converting the garage—which can be modified more easily than a room in regular use. A drip tray under the car engine will stop the floor becoming oily.

Good natural light is essential. Its potential can be maximized by using a white or silver reflector card to throw light onto that side of the subject that would otherwise be in shadow. White walls achieve the same effect, while the black wall provides a dark background, preventing stray light from spoiling shadow effects. In addition to natural light, electronic flash (either fitted to the camera or as an independent unit), photoflood bulbs in domestic fittings and tungsten filament studio lamps may be used.

Other useful elements include a table for laying out props and equipment; good ventilation and heating; plenty of power points; dust-proof storage cupboards; folding screen; mirror for making up; stool and step-ladder. The range of photographic equipment for studio use is large because you are not restricted by the need for portability or speed. The 35 mm camera has the advantage of being a good all-round system and the selection shown on the right contains all essential items for general use. Some professionals prefer bulky 12.5×10 cm (5×4 in) format cameras, which produce photographs of very high quality but have limited use in outdoor pictures. The 6×6 cm ($2\frac{1}{4}$ in sq) twin-lens reflex cameras such as Rolleiflex are a good size for portraits and may also be used outdoors. The tripod should be used in conjunction with the cable-release to eliminate shake caused by pressing the exposure button.

For the 35 mm user, the initial choice of supplementary lenses is usually a 28 mm wide-angle and a medium telephoto lens. Although the latter conventionally has a focal length of 135 mm, the shorter 85 mm or 105 mm lens is better for studio work because it allows closer focusing. Using a 135 mm lens for a full-length portrait, it is necessary to stand over six metres (twenty feet) from the subject.

A studio need not be a complicated set-up. Even a spare room or garage can be used. Add an appropriate background by pinning paper or material to a wall or hanging paper in the form of a roller. Effective lighting can be achieved using natural light from a window and a reflector card (left).

Mother and child (right) were photographed in a home studio, where I used a bedspread as background to give the picture added interest.

Accessories for a 35 mm system

1 Sturdy tripod.
2 Gadget bag. Ideally one that can be used from the shoulder.
3 Camera clamp.
4 Camera case. Not used if camera is packed in gadget bag.
5 Spare films. Always take more than needed of transparency, colour negative and black and white.
6 35 mm camera and standard lens.
7 Rigid lens case.
8 135 mm lens.
9 Gaffer (black) tape and masking tape.
10 Notebook and pen.
11 Cable release.
12 Lens hoods.
13 28 mm lens.
14 Lens caps.
15 Light meter.
16 Scissors and small screwdriver.
17 Dusting brush.
18 Clips.
19 Filters. Ultraviolet or 81A (preferably) and polarizing.
20 Portable reflector. Polystyrene ceiling tile or sheet of white card.
21 Neck strap.

Storage and presentation

A good storage system for photographic material is essential. The object is twofold—protection of work in good condition, and logical filing in a way that enables any given item to be retrieved efficiently.

Slides require particular care. They must be kept in a dry atmosphere in some form of dust-proof container. Avoid exposure to dampness or excessive heat. Normal room temperature is quite adequate for slide storage.

There are plenty of purpose-made storage aids available. Plastic viewpacks offer good protection, holding twenty slides in individual pockets. They are good for viewing a selection of transparencies simultaneously and may be stored in a deep filing drawer.

Special transparency boxes usually incorporate

an index card which corresponds with the numbered slots which hold the slides. If you have a magazine projector, slides can be stored in extra magazines. This is expensive and requires more storage space, but the material may be viewed immediately. Magazine storage is useful when the material falls into categories—for instance children at play, birthday parties or school sports days.

Negatives are best stored in strips, protected by special transparent or translucent bags. These may be kept in a negative cabinet with drawers, a filing cabinet or a loose-leaf album. A stationery ring-binder is ideal. Negatives are hard to judge at a glance—particularly those containing subtle detail—so it is sensible to make contact print sheets to be filed with the negatives for easy visual reference. Any prints that are not required for

display should be stored flat in a dry place.

It is important to label all material in some The information you choose to record shoul clude a brief description of the people and event, together with the date. This is espe relevant to photographs of children.

Mounted slides can be labelled with adhesive labels. Coloured stickers and self-adh numbers can identify categories or years. It course, possible to write directly on cardb slide mounts.

Negatives can be accompanied by technica formation. Attach the contact sheet to one si the negative bag with double-sided tape, lea the other free for noting information in ball-p pen or chinagraph pencil—though you must r write on a bag with negatives inside. I find

A contact sheet (left) makes it easier to evaluat the quality of negatives. Negatives and contact may be stored together in a special filing binde (above).

Viewpacks are ideal for storing slides. A numbe of slides may be viewed together without remov them, and the viewpack can be filed in a cabine Slides may be kept in spare projector magazine This method—though expensive—means that material is always ready for viewing, and can be useful if it falls into natural categories such as annual holidays.

developer and film used is usually sufficient, ...h I sometimes add paper grade. If trying to ...ct a particular technique, it can be useful to ...d additional information. The various results ...ved by changing, say, the shutter speed and ...ure can be analysed and compared. The over- ...dexing system is a matter of common sense. ...e are many methods and you should devise ...o suit your needs. The major consideration is ...ing that you can find what you're looking for ...vith minimal disruption.

...onsidering the effort that goes into the ...on of good photographs, it makes sense to ...similar pains with the presentation of your ...vork. Albums are the best way of displaying ...s as a collection. A little imagination can lift ...collection above the routine level of presenta-tion often seen in traditional family albums.

Avoid a regular arrangement of same-sized prints. Think of the album as a magazine and attempt to design the pages to achieve magazine-style impact, even to the extent of producing headlines with instant lettering. Create a photo-graphic diary—a visually-stimulating mixture of photographs and written commentary. With modern adhesives you can try alternative arrange-ments, lifting and repositioning prints until the desired result is attained.

For a more flexible—and decorative—display, a collage of child photographs mounted with pins on a cork notice-board can be effective, as can single montages of different prints. It is interesting, for example, to form a montage featuring a growing child over the years.

Dry-mounting is the best method for exhibit-ing prints, framed or otherwise, and is not com-plicated. Dry-mounting tissue, domestic iron and mounting board are required. Tack the shiny side of the tissue to the back of the print with the tip of a warm iron, not pressing too hard; trim tissue to size with scissors or trimming knife; place the print, tissue downwards, on pre-cut mounting board; cover surface of print with a sheet of clean thick paper and, using iron at medium heat, keep it moving over print for thirty seconds, applying firm pressure. Add hardboard base, glass and clips for a print that is ready to hang.

I prefer to use grey card for mounting. This tones with the print and enhances the overall effect, while the more popular black or white can create unnecessary conflict.

Photomontage is an exciting technique that can produce excellent and original results. It involves the combina-tion of individual prints into a composite whole, and provides endless scope for creativity. There are certain basic rules to follow. I use prints on single-weight, matt paper for ease of cutting and retouching. Expressions should either harmonize or be in complete contrast for added effect. The originals should be lit in a similar way to ensure consistency of shadow and highlight. In the example shown, the portraits of the three children have been cut out and super-imposed on a base print of the family home. Before gluing the cut-outs in position I bevelled the cut edges with fine sandpaper and blacked the edges with pencil to disguise the join before pasting down. Once in place, the job was finished by retouching the boy's knee black and re-shooting the whole with a standard lens. Photomontage can be seen as a jigsaw puzzle in which you place the pieces where you like. Enlarge or reduce elements if you wish, or consider using the same subject several times. A child with varied expressions—or at different ages—can make an excellent and amusing montage.

Applying the photographer's skills

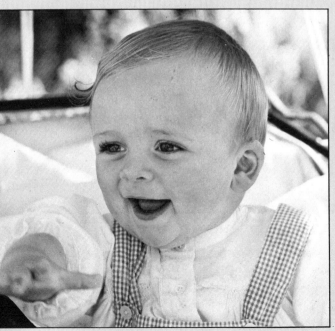

Introduction

Mastery of the basic skills of the photographer does not involve a long and painful apprenticeship. Obviously, the more you practise and look at your results with a critical eye the more confidently you will handle your equipment and react to the photographic possibilities of a situation. What every photographer should be aiming for is an instinctive response to the exciting potential that children provide. The first essential, therefore, is to have the camera ready to hand and loaded.

Applying the photographer's skills to the subject of children requires as much understanding of the way they behave and react as of the techniques of photography. A little experience will quickly show you how the characteristics of children—their spontaneity, their vitality, their rapid changes of mood and their relatively short spans of interest—give wonderful opportunities for exciting photographs while compelling you to be adaptable in the way you go about taking photographs. Success does not necessarily depend on capturing dramatic or important moments but it does mean being ready to seize an expression or a gesture the moment it comes. There are few other fields of photography where you have to be as alert and attentive if you are to convey the essence of a moment.

In this section, I have covered the essential aspects of choosing exposure, depth of field, shutter speed and selecting film. I have also dealt with the way to use three different types of lenses: telephoto, wide-angle and zoom. Underlying this is my own preference for 35 mm single-lens reflex cameras that will take interchangeable lenses. Without being prohibitively expensive, they do provide the photographer with exceptionally versatile camera systems. However, my own preference should not discourage you if you want to spend less money on your equipment. Particularly for the beginner, it is a great mistake to be burdened with equipment you have not the confidence to use.

I have concluded this section by looking at the way the photographer works in different lighting conditions, including a simple studio. Studio lighting may sound forbiddingly professional but it is surprising how easily a temporary studio can be set up in the home.

Working out exposure

Choosing the right exposure is as much art as science, and no meter can tell the photographer what his choice should be. None the less, the decision must be based on accurate knowledge of the brightness of the subject provided by a hand-held or built-in meter.

Often there is more contrast in a scene than your film can handle, and some part of the scene will then need to be under- or overexposed. One of the commonest pitfalls is presented by a bright sky behind the subject. The bright sky could mislead the meter into indicating a smaller exposure than is needed, and the figures would end up as silhouettes. On the other hand, children in sunlight seen against a deep shadow might be overexposed because the dark background dominates the meter's reading.

There are several ways to exclude a misleading background: you can move up close to the subject while you set the exposure, and then step back to take the shot; you can take the reading while pointing the camera at some other part of the scene that has the desired brightness (for example, you can exclude the sky by tilting the camera downwards, at the foreground, while setting the exposure); or you can take a reading from your own hand (assuming that flesh tones are the most important part of the subject, and that your hand is in similar lighting conditions).

It is important to know whether a built-in meter averages the brightness of all parts of the scene, or whether it is centre-weighted—that is, whether the reading depends mainly on the brightness of the central part of the scene. Centre-weighting is undoubtedly an advantage for rapid shooting, but a centre-weighted meter must be used with care when the main subject is off centre. It may be necessary to aim the camera at the subject to take the reading and then set the shutter before shifting the angle of view to take the picture.

A mother and her make a delightful sequence of photographs shot within limited environme the home. Even in conditions, the pro lems of arriving at correct exposure v considerably. By posing them in an exterior doorway (and exposing for th highlight, I have fr the figures and iso them against the d interior. In the sam way, for the photog of them playing together on a velve covered sofa, I hav exposed for the hig light so that the co plicated setting is relative darkness. order to convey the freshness of a sun room (opposite), I exposed for the sh area and allowed h lights, such as the windows, to burn c This element of ov exposure has help create the impress of airy spaciousne

The area from which to take an exposure reading is that part of the scene on which you wish to concentrate—possibly quite a small part of the whole. In a picture of children outlined against the sky, for example, if you want to emphasize the detail of the clouds and reduce the figures to silhouettes, take a reading from the sky and expose for that. For detail in the figures, take a close-up reading from them and expose accordingly.

If, for a high-contrast scene such as a sunset, your meter gives an averaged reading, then the setting it indicates will overexpose the extremely light areas and underexpose the extremely dark areas. If you reduce the exposure by one or two stops from the indicated reading, there will be detail in the clouds and the landscape will be sombre, creating a "midnight sun" effect. If you increase the exposure by a stop, the image of the sun will be burned out and the landscape will have a daytime look. This is a striking example of how exercising your judgement can create alternative but equally valid interpretations.

Errors in exposure may not be serious when you are using black and white film: a variation of plus or minus one stop may give an adequate negative. Colour negative film must be more accurately exposed to about half a stop. In both cases, corrections for faulty exposure can be made at the printing stage. In fact, prints you send to ordinary commercial processors are automatically corrected to a small degree.

In the case of colour transparencies, however, an error of one-half stop in exposure is the most that can be tolerated, and that only in special circumstances. If in doubt, experienced photographers usually bracket their exposure.

Diffused lighting (below) allows exposures that record a range of tones and subtleties of texture. *Rolleiflex, 1/125, f8, Tri-X.*

The dramatic silhouettes of father and son (right) were achieved by exposing for the sky. *Hasselblad, 80 mm, 1/500, f11, Tri-X, yellow filter.*

Contrast problems are accentuated when a bright light source such as a low sun (opposite) is included. Here, the lake provides fill-in light. *Hasselblad, 80 mm, 1/250, f8, Tri-X, yellow filter.*

Controlling depth of field

Applying the photographer's skills

Controlling the aperture to change the depth of field adds a vital dimension to your photographs and is really as simple as it is important. The fundamental rule is, the smaller the aperture, the greater the depth of field, other things being equal. When focusing your camera by setting it against a fixed reference mark, you will notice that on each side of that mark is a series of calibration lines, each line corresponding to a certain aperture.

The f4 calibration line on one side marks the farthest distance at which subjects are sharply focused when the aperture is set at f4, while its counterpart on the other side indicates the minimum distance. Try varying the focus setting: the f4 calibrations indicate a smaller depth of field as you focus on closer images. So your focusing has to be more precise when you're shooting close-ups. Comparing scales on different types of

lenses will show you that wide-angle (short-focal length) lenses have greater depth of field than standard lenses; telephoto (long focal length) lenses have a much shallower depth of field. To get the best out of different types of lenses, an understanding of these characteristics is as important as an appreciation of the angle of view.

You must be sufficiently familiar with the control of the depth of field to be able to make a conscious choice concerning it for every picture. Do you want as much as possible of the foreground and background in focus? This might be the case if you are photographing an extended group of subjects—some children near the camera, some farther from it—in order to make an interesting composition. In this case, set the smallest possible aperture. But remember that the shutter speed will need to be correspondingly slower, and if it is too slow you

run the risk of blur due to camera shake or sub movement. On the other hand, you may wis keep a distracting background or foreground of focus in order to concentrate attention on subject. Then you need the largest aperture p ible, and a faster shutter speed to compensate.

Use the maximum depth of field when want to be ready to shoot unpredictable subjec a moment's notice. Choose the smallest aper that conditions permit and set the infinity mar the focusing ring just inside the upper mark corresponding to that aperture on the depth field scale. Your depth of field will now ext from infinity down to some relatively close po and only minor adjustments will be needed fo but very close subjects. With your camera se this way you can photograph active chil without having to adjust the focus for each shot

Distance scale (ft and metres)

Depth-of-field scale (zone in focus)

A standard lens for a 35 mm camera, set at an aperture of f4, shows the depth of field by calibrations that are read against the focusing ring. The zone of sharp focus decreases the closer the lens is focused. The depth of field is extended when the aperture is reduced from f4 to f16 (right).

f4 — Zone in focus

| Metres | 1 | 2 | 3 | 4 | 5 |
| Feet | 3 | 6 | 9 | 12 | 15 |

f16 — Zone in focus

In these three pictur for all of which I use a 35 mm camera fitte with a standard lens depth of field has be used to enhance composition.

An open aperture o f2.8 allowed me to record the little boy left) so that he is cle defined while the ba ground is sufficient diffused for it not to be distracting.

The silhouettes of t boys standing in a doorway (left) provic an unusual frame fo Thai palace. I stopp down to f22 to get ar acceptable degree sharpness over a maximum distance

The bizarre pose of smiling contortionis (right) is all the mor striking because it i seen in conjunction a boy standing normally. To concentrate attention o the girl, I used a wic aperture, exploiting different definition the two figures.

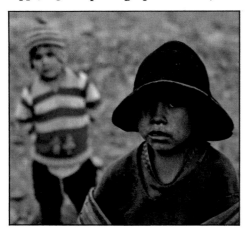

Though altering the aperture is a relatively simple technical adjustment, controlling the depth of field in this way is a crucial factor in getting the image you want. Varying the depth of field does not simply increase or decrease the area of image in sharp focus; it can modify the compositional, colour, tonal and light values of a picture.

The effect of manipulating aperture is well demonstrated by this pair of photographs of Peruvian boys, shot through the open window of a stationary car on the outskirts of Cuzco. Both photographs were taken with high-speed film, which gives the additional flexibility particularly useful in conditions of mixed light and shade. In taking the photograph above, I followed the basic rule of shooting to capture the telling image without losing time on fine adjustments of settings. If you have time to take more photographs, then that is your opportunity to see how you might improve the image by, for instance, changing the depth of field. Though I wanted the solid presence of the boy in the black hat to be the dominant element, I felt it could be juxtaposed against the bright clothing of his friend. However, in this photograph I have used maximum depth of field so that the boy in the background in his multi-coloured sweater overpowers the sombre subtleties of the boy in the foreground. *Pentax, 50 mm, 1/125, f16, Ektachrome 400.*

As the children were holding their pose, I quickly altered the aperture to f5.6 at 1/1000 second. This adjustment has considerably enhanced the composition and the aesthetic values of the picture. The reduction in the depth of field has resulted in the enlargement of the background figure, the softening of background colour, the merging of highlight and shadow areas, and the toning down of all background detail. The boy in the foreground now looms out of the picture, indisputably the dominant element. The subdued background colour intensifies the colour of his clothing and, rather than being a distraction, the background figure has become an effective foil, though fully integrated with the foreground.

Selecting shutter speed

By using a fast shutter speed, 1/500 second or faster, it is possible to "freeze" the rapid movements of children playing. Slower shutter speeds may record the same activities with blur. Provided the use of blur is controlled, it can powerfully convey a sense of movement. Fast shutter speeds are, however, very useful if you want to record the highly energetic behaviour of children. Fast film used in conjunction with fast shutter speeds allows you to stop down the aperture and record a reasonable depth of field.

In selecting the shutter speed for the effect you want, you must take into account distance from camera to subject and the direction of movement, as well as the speed at which the subject is travelling. A subject moving at a constant speed requires a faster shutter speed to "freeze" its movement the closer it is to the camera. As the table on page 39 shows, when a subject is moving at an oblique angle towards the camera, a faster shutter speed is needed to stop movement than when it is coming directly towards the camera. An even faster speed is needed to stop movement when the subject is travelling parallel to the plane of the camera.

Fast shutter speeds also help to eliminate camera shake, which probably spoils more pictures than any other factor. In unskilled hands, 1/125 second is probably the safest choice. With practice and in calm conditions, it is quite easy to produce second. But if you are badly balanced, or photographing in wind, use the highest possible speed consistent with available light.

Medium shutter speeds were used for the boy with the cat and the cartwheeling girl. The boy presented nothing problematic in terms of depth of field or movement and, by choosing 1/60, I was able to get enough depth of field to make both subjects sharp and to stop any movement likely to be made. I wanted to capture the girl's cartwheel at its climax in order to express the nature of the activity. I chose a speed of 1/125 because stopping the movement completely would have made the image look like a cut-out.

Slow shutter speeds were deliberately chosen for the girl playing blindman's bluff (below). I wanted to capture the instant when the girl was pausing, the static moment in a turbulent game. At 1/15, she is acceptably sharp, but the other children record as blurs. A faster speed would have frozen all movement but at the expense of atmosphere and immediacy. The boy being showered (right) was shot at 1/30 so the flow of water recorded as a continuous stream.

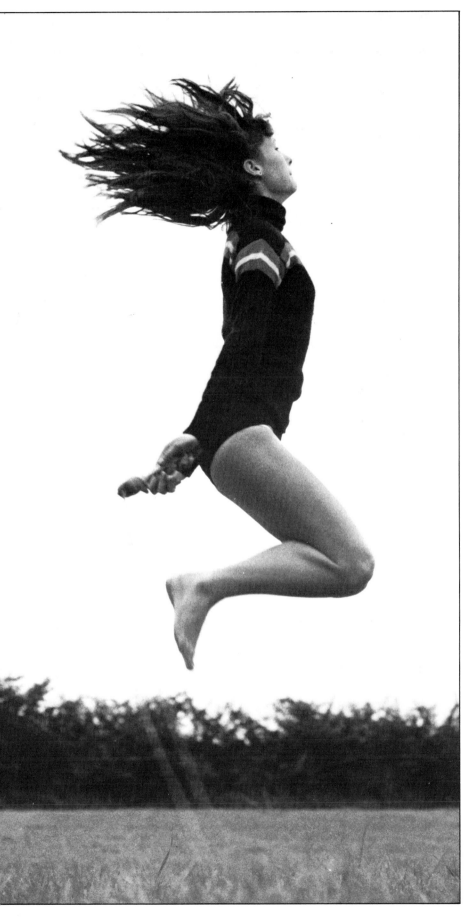

By setting stopped action against plain backgrounds, interesting shapes can be given strong emphasis. I was taken with the girl's ability (left) to jump high when skipping and with her beautiful, floating hair. I shot from a low angle to record her clearly against the sky. As I exposed at the jump's climax, 1/250 was enough to freeze most of the movement. To stop the movement of the little boy (below). I used a speed of 1/500.

Use the camera on a tripod if there is risk of camera shake— generally at any speed less than 1/60. If without a tripod, rest the camera, or brace yourself on something solid; squeeze the release gently.

Choosing the right shutter speed

Experience is the only way to judge accurately the shutter speed needed to stop an action, but the following table is a useful guide. Apparent speed changes not only with the direction in which the subject is moving, but with how far it is from the camera, and the type of lens in use. This table assumes that the subject is photographed in the middle distance with a standard lens.

Subject	Towards	Diagonally	Across
Portrait	1/60	—	—
Walking	1/30	1/60	1/125
Cycling	1/60	1/125	1/250
Swimming	1/250	1/500	1/1000
Running	1/500	1/1000	1/1000

39

Applying the photographer's skills/SELECTING SHUTTER SPEED

The energy and volatile moods of children make them endlessly fascinating subjects. Fast films and the fast lenses of modern cameras allow the photographer to pluck an instant from a fast-moving sequence and record it in crisp detail. However, there is no "right" shutter speed for a given situation. An image containing the blur of movement can convey the excitement and liveliness of children with more spontaneity and force than an image with all movement frozen.

Tantrums and tears are just as much a part of childhood as smiles and contentment. I wanted to convey the violence of this little girl's outburst, as she screamed and shook her head wildly from side to side. The camera was pre-set at a shutter speed of 1/250, clearly insufficient to freeze the movement but not so slow that the impassioned momentary rage records as a total blur. The result is a picture that successfully captures powerful emotion. *Pentax, 135 mm, 1/250, f8, Ektachrome 64.*

The whirling figure of the skateboarder was travelling at such speed that in the restricted of the rink I could not follow him through with camera. I wanted to arrest the movement so as record the shape and form of the figure as it hurtled round the rim of the bowl. I pre-focuse a fixed position and used the fastest speed available. Fast film enabled me to close down aperture and record a maximum depth of field *Pentax, 50 mm, 1/1000, f16, Ektachrome 200.*

The choice of film

6 × 6 cm
(2¼ in sq)

24 × 36 mm

13 × 17 mm

120

35 mm

110

The sizes of film most used are 120 and 220 roll film, 35 mm cassettes and 110 cartridges. With 120 roll film there are 12 exposures and with 220 there are 24 exposures, both of 6 × 6 cm (2¼ in sq). Some cameras take 15 exposures on a 120 at 6 × 4.5 cm (2¼ × 1¾ in). Whereas 120 film has protective backing paper for its entire length, 220 has only a short trailer. Cassettes of 35 mm film come in 20, 24 and 36 exposures and are rewound before opening the camera. Drop-in cartridges of 110 in 12 or 20 exposures are not rewound.

The type of camera you own determines the type of film you use. The subject you wish to photograph, the lighting conditions, and whether you want to produce black and white prints, colour prints or colour slides determine the type of film you use. Black and white and colour negatives produce negatives which have to be subsequently printed to give positive paper prints. With colour transparency film there are no negatives; the end result is the actual film on which you made the exposure. Colour prints can be made from colour slides or transparencies, but the results are not as satisfactory as prints made from negatives. Colour transparency films are available for daylight or artificial light and the correct film should be used for accurate colour representation.

Films are also available in different speed ratings, which are measured in ASA or DIN. Both of these are gradually being replaced by ISO, a universally acceptable set of film-speed standards. For example, a film with a rating ASA 400/27 DIN will be expressed in the rating ISO 400/27°. Film speed is the sensitivity or speed with which a

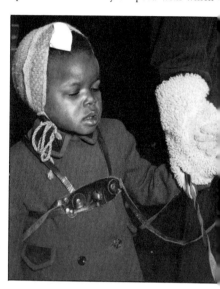

The face of a shy child holding her mother's hand provides a strong contrast to the white glove. The picture was taken on Plus-X film which has admirably represented the tonal range from black to white and the subtleties of texture in the child's clothing.

A sensitive portrait of this beautiful young girl is enhanced by the fine grained film in this picture. I used Panatomic-X which reproduced the even black of the background as well as the delicate textures of the girl's clothes and hair. The light was diffused daylight which also revealed the quality of her complexion.

An atmosphere of romance and mystery has been created by taking this photograph in the available light cast by a candle. Taken on a fast film (Tri-X) this picture has a coarse grain but also a high contrast because of the harsh lighting conditions. There is some loss of detail in the highlights and tone in the girl's face.

s to light. A film with a rating of 400 ASA is
: film, and a film with a rating of 25 ASA is a
film. Under identical lighting conditions a
film requires a shorter exposure than a slow
to produce a similar result.

As a reminder of the type of film in your
era, it is always a good idea when loading, to
off the end flap of the film carton and either
it into the camera case, or tape it onto the
era back.

Normal film speeds, that is, the film speeds for
age conditions, are 125 ASA for black and
te, 100 ASA for colour negative and 64 ASA
colour transparency. Fast films are a valuable
to the photographer, enabling pictures to be
n with available light where previously flash
ld have been necessary, but remember that a
film may not always be the one you need. It is
uch a disadvantage to try to photograph under
bright lighting conditions with a fast film as
to try to photograph under very poor lighting
ditions with a slow one.

Grain and contrast are also associated with film
speed. The faster a film, the coarser the grain and
the lower the contrast of the emulsion; there is,
however, more exposure latitude with faster films.
With fast colour films there is also a loss of colour
accuracy, but grain can be used to good effect, and
the colour, although less accurate, is not un-
attractive.

Most colour transparency films are balanced
for exposure in average daylight and a yellow to
amber overall cast will result when they are used
with tungsten filament (domestic and photoflood) lamps. This can be corrected with the use
of the appropriate bluish conversion filter; an 80A
for domestic light and an 80B for photoflood
lamps. Unfortunately, these filters also reduce the
effective speed of the film by 2 and $1\frac{2}{3}$ stops respectively. A better solution is to use a type B film
specifically designed for tungsten light, such as
Ektachrome ET 160. Type B materials can also be
exposed in daylight using an 85B amber filter with
a speed loss of $\frac{2}{3}$ of a stop. This information is for
producing colour correct transparencies. Interesting special effects can be obtained by taking photo-

graphs in incorrect or mixed lighting. Fluorescent
light is not suitable for colour correct photography
because it is deficient in certain wavelengths of
light. Fairly satisfactory results can be obtained by
using daylight film, although they tend to have a
bluish-green bias.

Choosing a brand of film is largely a matter of
convenience and personal preference because they
are all of a high standard, but it is a good idea to
experiment to find the ones you like and stick to
them.

When buying film, always check the expiry
date printed on the side of the carton so that you
do not buy film with only a short life. When buying a quantity of colour transparency films also
look for the batch number and try to buy them all
from the same batch. This is because the speed and
colour bias of colour materials vary from batch
to batch. With Ektachrome in particular you
should note the instructions packed with each film
in which the precise speed is given in red. In this
way you will avoid having to alter your camera
every time you change the film.

FILMS

Film name	ASA	Sizes
BLACK AND WHITE NEGATIVE FILMS		
Ilford		
Pan F	50	135-20, 135-36, 35 mm (reloads) bulk film, 120, 220
FP4	125	135-20, 135-36, 35 mm (reloads) bulk film, 120, 220
HP5	400	135-20, 135-36, 35 mm (reloads) bulk film, 120, 220
Kodak		
Panatomic-X	32	135-36, 35 mm (reloads) bulk film
Panatomic-X Professional	32	120
Plus-X Pan	125	135-20, 135-36, 35 mm (reloads) bulk film
Verichrome Pan	125	110-12, 126-12, 126-20, 35 mm (reloads) bulk film, 120
Tri-X Pan	400	135-20, 135-36, 35 mm (reloads) bulk film, 120
Royal-X Pan	1250	120
COLOUR NEGATIVE FILMS		
Agfacolor CNS	80	126-12, 126-20, 135-12, 135-20, 135-36, 120
Agfacolor CN110	80	110-12, 110-20
Agfacolor CNS	400	110-12, 110-20, 135-24, 135-36
Fujicolor F-11	100	110-12, 110-24, 126-24, 126-24, 135-24, 135-36, 120
Fujicolor F-II 400	400	110-12, 110-24, 135-24, 135-36, 120
Kodacolor II	100	110-12, 110-20, 126-12, 126-20, 135-12, 135-24, 135-36, 120
Kodacolor 400	400	110-12, 110-20, 135-12, 135-24, 135-36, 120
Sakuracolor II	100	110-12, 110-24, 126-12, 126-20, 135-12, 135-24, 135-36, 120
Sakuracolor 400	400	110-12, 110-24, 135-24, 135-36, 120
COLOUR TRANSPARENCY FILMS		
Agfacolor CT 18 (Daylight)	50	135-20, 135-36, 120
Agfachrome 50S (Daylight)	50	135-36, 120
50L (Tungsten)		
Agfacolor CT110 (Daylight)	64	110-20
Agfacolor CT126 (Daylight)	64	126-20
Agfacolor CT21 (Daylight)	100	135-36
Agfachrome 100 Professional (Daylight)	100	135-36
Fujichrome RD100 (Daylight)	100	135-20, 135-36
Kodachrome 25 (Daylight)	25	135-20, 135-36
Kodachrome 64 (Daylight)	64	110-20, 126-20, 135-20, 135-36
Ektachrome 64 (Daylight)	64	110-20, 126-20, 135-20, 135-36, 120
Ektachrome 160 (Tungsten)	160	135-20, 135-36
Ektachrome 200 (Daylight)	200	135-20, 135-36
Ektachrome 200 Professional (Daylight)	200	120, 135-36
Ektachrome 400 (Daylight)	400	135-20, 135-36, 120

135 is the code for 35 mm film
135-36 reloads are lengths of film for reloadable 35 mm film cassettes

43

Film is by definition a sensitive material and it needs careful storage in a cool dry place. A domestic fridge is ideal but you must allow one hour before opening the foil wrapping, otherwise condensation will occur. Films should be processed as soon as possible after exposure and kept cool and dry until that opportunity arises. Some films made for the amateur market, such as Kodachrome, are designed to survive various storage conditions before and after exposure without loss of colour balance, whereas Ektachrome, primarily a professional film, is designed to be exposed and processed in a short space of time.

Commercial colour processing is mostly auto-mated and thus consistent but, because it aims only to produce a good average result from a good average light and exposure situation, it is often worth bracketing your exposure to be sure.

Although acceptable when processed commercially, black and white films are very easy to process yourself and the results can be much better. It also extends your control of the photograph from conception to final print.

The cool muted tones of a Peruvian girl in Lima (left) and the glowing, warm tones of a tanned sunbather (below) clearly illustrate the range of tones and colours modern colour film can achieve. *(Left) Pentax, 100 mm, 1/250, f5.6, Kodachrome 64.*

The negative (left) is the final processing stage before printing onto paper (below). The colours are com-plementary; yellow appears where blue will be, magenta for green and cyan for red. *Pentax, 100 mm, 1/125, f8, Kodachrome 64.*

Working with a telephoto lens

135 mm f3.5

Telephoto lenses are heavy. To avoid camera shake, use a tripod or, if the camera is hand-held, brace yourself firmly and support lens as well as camera body.

Telephoto lenses bring a distant subject closer by magnifying the image size. The longer the focal length, the narrower the field of view: a 50 mm lens gives an angle of view of 46°, a 135 mm one of 18°, while a 400 mm lens covers as little as 6°. Accordingly, as the focal length increases, less of the subject appears in the viewfinder.

Being able to stand at some distance from the subject while still filling the frame is obviously a great advantage if the subject is at all camera-shy. Many people, adults as well as children, are acutely conscious of a camera being aimed at them from close in, and this inhibits their behaviour. With the photographer at a safe distance, they can relax, and better pictures will result. Candid shots, taken without the subject's knowledge, are also easier when working inconspicuously from a distance with a telephoto lens.

The visual properties of a telephoto lens make it a useful tool for photographing people. The most noticeable is the compression of space, which draws the background more closely in on the foreground and alters our perception of apparent space between objects. The longer the focal length, the more spectacular this effect becomes.

The limited depth of field of a telephoto lens enables the photographer, by judicious focusing, to blur out a distracting background. Using a 135 mm lens set, for example, at f4 and focused sharply on a child 3 m (10 ft) away, anything behind the child will be increasingly out of focus, and the main subject will stand out crisply against this blurred background. Details between the subject and the photographer will also be out of focus. Such elements can be deliberately introduced to give depth to the composition, or to add a splash abstract colour. This technique of different focusing needs careful checking with the dep of-field preview facility on the lens or by manu stopping down to the taking aperture.

Telephoto lenses come in a wide range focal lengths, from about 85 mm to 1000 mm beyond. A 2× tele-converter, an extra set elements placed between camera and lens, useful accessory, effectively doubling the f length but demanding extra exposure. Av cheap models, whose optical quality can be po The "portrait" lens of between 85 and 105 is a very useful one to work with: it enables photographer to fill the frame for a head-a shoulders shot without being uncomfortably c to his subject, does not distort facial features, is not too strong a lens to use in the confined sp of the average room. Outdoors, where distan are greater, the more powerful 135 mm co into its own. In general, though, a lens wit focal length of more than 200 mm will be strong to have more than a very limited appl tion in child portraiture.

Telephoto lenses are longer and heavier t those of shorter focal length, and a faster minim shutter speed has to be used to avoid camera sha Though you can sometimes get away with slo speeds, try shooting with a hand-held 135 mm at no slower than 1/125 second, 1/250 second f 200 mm, 1/500 second for a 500 mm, and so or conditions prevent this, brace yourself firr against a wall or use a tripod and cable releas with the longest lenses this will be necessary any case.

A Hebridean scene recorded with a normal lens (above) includes a lot of foreground. Using a 135 mm telephoto lens (right) allowed me to fill the frame with the main subject. At the same time, it has brought up the background, so that the image conveys the harsh isolation of this small group.

50 mm

135 mm

The three frames indicate the areas of the picture that would be covered by three lenses of different focal length if the photographer remains in the same position. These three are applicable to 35 mm cameras but other cameras taking interchangeable lenses have comparable ranges. The photograph has been taken with a 28 mm wide-angle and the middle frame shows the area covered by a 50 mm lens, a standard lens for a 35 mm camera. The central frame picks out the area that would be covered by a 135 mm lens, that is a medium telephoto. The effect on depth of field and compression of space would be different with each lens.

135 mm

50 mm

28 mm

The antics of a child showing off and trying to distract me needed to be photographed from a distance if I was not to shatter the boy's mood. Using a 135 mm lens enabled me to fill the frame with my subject and to capture the facial expression while having sufficient room to work.

The great advantage of telephoto lenses is that they allow the photographer to stand at a distance from his subject and yet record a sizeable image. Even a medium telephoto lens brings within the camera's capabilities a vast range of pictures which otherwise would be inaccessible. These lenses are particularly useful in photographing children, who easily become self-conscious when the camera is brought close in.

An intimate portrait of the girl and her pet rabbit was possible from a distance of about 10 metres using a fairly long telephoto lens. The limited depth of field has simplified both background and foreground, the shades of pastel green suggesting the atmosphere of a lush garden. *Leicaflex, 400 mm, 1/1000, f8, Ektachrome 200.*

A medium telephoto lens enabled me to capture the delight of this little girl and to isolate her and her shadow against the gentle wash of the sea. By taking up a vantage point on a beach and using a telephoto lens, it is possible to remain inconspicuous while recording the spontaneous play of children. *Pentax, 135 mm, 1/250, f8, Ektachrome 64.*

Using a wide-angle lens

28 mm

In comparison with standard lenses, wide-angle lenses have shorter focal lengths and take in a greater field of view. On a 35 mm camera, the focal length of a standard lens is usually 50 or 55 mm and its angle of view, about 50° or 45° respectively, is roughly equivalent to that of the human eye. Wide-angle lenses for 35 mm cameras are usually made in focal lengths of 35 mm, 28 mm, 24 mm, 21 mm, 18 mm, 15 mm and 8 mm or 6 mm, their angle of view ranging from 63° to 220°. The first three are the most commonly used, significantly increasing the angle of view in comparison with a standard lens without introducing an unacceptable degree of distortion. The last two are ultra-wide-angle or fisheye lenses with an angle of view of 180° or more. On a 6 × 6 cm (2¼ in sq) format camera, the standard lens usually has a

focal length of 80 mm and the medium w angle 50 or 55 mm, with shorter focal le available in certain cases.

Wide-angles come into their own when pl graphing landscapes or interiors and, more ticularly, people or groups in their environm Apart from simply getting more into the fr the wide-angle makes these subjects look cramped than a standard lens would and cor the relationship of foreground to far dist whereas the standard lens tends to relate m distance to infinity. This is partly because the v angle covers not only the eye's main field of v but also some of its peripheral vision—in words what is "half" seen out of the corners c eyes. People are often disappointed that some of a scene that had a certain prominence when

The piper has bee photographed with wide-angle lens to convey his relation at a position in the middle distance, to vast field of lush gr emphasized by the inclusion of so muc foreground.

The fighting boys occupy a dominant position in the fore ground but the bro depth of field allow striking contrast w distant group of mc orderly boys. With standard lens, I wo have had to stand further from the fig ing boys to get ther the frame and the picture would have less impact.

The cyclists prepa for a race were so hemmed in by the crowd that a wide- angle lens was nee to get these boys in the frame and all in focus. The dramati angle of view has g a feeling of immed to this moment just before the race.

Distortion within acceptable limits c make a picture mor forceful. A 28 mm l used in this close-u a girl at a party has exaggerated the si the hand she is usi to spoon food into h mouth. The distort is not overdone but enough to suggest hearty appetite.

the eyes is either cut out entirely or appears ...ificant in a photograph taken with a standard ... The wide-angle goes some way to solving ...roblem—a particular advantage when fore-...ds are concerned because they often have an ...rtant relationship with other parts of the ...re.

...he second key feature of the wide-angle is the ...er depth of field it gives compared with a ...ard lens. At a given aperture and distance, a ...-angle lens will give far greater depth of field ...will a 50 mm standard lens. This is an advan-...when sharp focus is wanted over a long ...ce, but a drawback when selective focusing ...ded.

...wide-angle lens also affects scale, making ...cts in the foreground appear large compared with those in the middle or far distance. At its most marked, this becomes distortion. Although distortion can be used to create a certain atmo-sphere and, especially, a sense of immediacy when there are people or objects in the foreground, it is easily overdone and should be treated with respect.

Added control of perspective is given by using a wide-angle and this is useful when working in confined spaces: quite a small change in camera position produces a comparatively large change in viewpoint.

Some people find the choice between a 35 mm and a 28 mm wide-angle difficult to make. I prefer the 28 mm lens because, if used with discretion, most results are acceptably free of distortion and the wider angle of view does open up more possi-bilities. A 35 mm gives a "truer" result and for this reason is preferred in photojournalism.

The ultra-wide-angles, otherwise called fish-eyes, should be treated with caution: they distort all straight lines into curves, producing a round image. While this is a distinctive effect, it soon becomes boring if used too often. With a fisheye it is possible to achieve angles of view up to 220° but, because they need many more elements than a standard or long lens, good fisheyes are expensive.

Conventional wide-angles are compact and easy to hold and, although slower than standard lenses, are now being made with much wider maximum apertures than they used to be and can cope with most lighting conditions. Although more expensive than standard lenses, they are a vital acquisition for the photographer who wants to expand his capabilities.

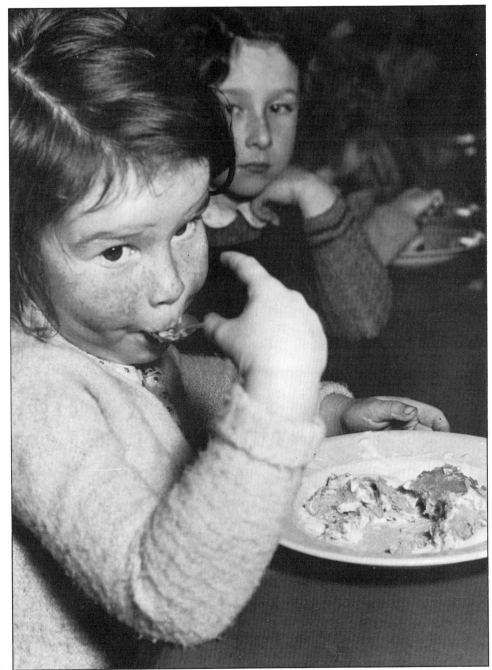

Children's rooms, the territories that children consider their own, provide settings that express a great deal about character and interests. A wide-angle lens will be necessary unless you want to photograph just a small area. Using a standard lens in this study, the image includes only the boy at his desk and a limited background, which gives an impression of a neat, well-organized room. By using a wide-angle lens, I have recorded the whole room, enlarging foreground features and so emphasizing the characteristic muddle of a teenage boy. *Pentax, 28 mm, 1/60, f5.6, Ektachrome 200.*

Close-up portraits with wide-angle lenses show a degree of distortion but, provided this is not excessive, it can help create interesting pictures. In this adult's-eye view of a child, the distortion has helped create an arresting image, the eyes at the centre point providing a direct contact that offsets the exaggeration of the head. Choose the angle of view carefully and, for close-ups, limit the lens to a medium wide-angle: ultra-wide lenses give unacceptable distortion. *Pentax, 28 mm, 1/250, f5.6, Ektachrome 200.*

The advantages of a zoom lens

Vivitar 35–70 mm

Vivitar 70–210 mm

The major benefits of a zoom lens are the choice of focal lengths it offers and the ease and increased subtlety with which pictures can be framed in comparison with lenses of fixed focal length. A zoom does the job of two or more separate lenses, so you don't have to change lenses as often or carry so much equipment around. A 35–70 mm zoom lens extends the range of a normal (50 mm) lens to cover both moderate wide-angle and long lens work, while a 70–210 mm ranges from a "portrait" lens to a much more powerful telephoto with, of course, infinite variations within this range. They are more expensive than a conventional lens but cheaper by far than the three separate fixed focal length lenses whose basic functions they replace. Less time is lost changing lenses and many offer macro (close-focus) facilities.

The lens is focused in the normal way, and it will remain in focus no matter how the focal length is varied. Standing in a fixed position, the photographer can move in close to his subject by extending the lens towards its maximum focal length, or pull back for a wider shot, until the ideal composition presents itself. A zoom lens also enables him to maintain the image size of the subject as the child moves to and fro in front of the camera, though, as the subject-camera distance is now changing, refocusing will be necessary. On modern one-touch zooms this is simplified by combining the controls for focus and for focal length—the lens barrel is rotated to focus and

moved in or out to adjust focal length. Old models have separate rings for these functions, a two distinct movements are needed. With a zoo there is thus no need for the photographer to d back and forth following his subject—he can sta still and let the lens do the moving for him. Spec effects are possible too: focus on a subject filling more than half the frame and set the lens at longest focal length. Then, while the shutter open (a slow speed will be necessary), zoom ba in to get a rushing effect of speed and moveme Experiment with different combinations of posure and zoom as this is not the easiest techni to master.

Most good modern zoom lenses are of eq optical quality to fixed lenses, though this can be said of older or cheaper models. There are advantages, however. Zooms are more comp optically and there is thus more to go wrong as lens elements loosen up with use. Their length a weight are greater than an equivalent fixed lens use a higher shutter speed or a tripod to av camera shake (test-exposing a few frames of f will soon show you the minimum speed at wh you can *consistently* hold the camera steady). T maximum aperture is rarely less than around Most fixed lenses go at least one stop beyond t and so a zoom is more limited for low-light wo But for many photographic situations, particula if only one lens is to be carried, the flexibility the zoom lens far outweighs these disadvantage

Taken with a 70-210 mm zoom at its shortest focal length from five metres, father and son are too small in the frame for any features to be revealed. The distracting background prevents a sympathetic composition without a different viewpoint.

By setting the zoom at a focal length of 150 mm I was able to cut out the background and close in on my subjects to show both their expressions and the subdued mood that characterized their relationship. All the important elements are retained.

For the third shot I u the zoom just short its maximum focal length of 210 mm. T frame is filled with t heads of father and child. All distractin detail in the back-ground has now be lost and attention is on their features.

Zooming during exposure requires experience if you are to get a smooth movement in changing the focal length of the lens. In general, it is best to zoom at the slowest speed that is consistent with the amount of light, the speed of the film and your ability to hold the camera steady.

Trainee bullfighters in Lima, boys of sixteen, practise their elegant and dangerous passes with a skeletal wheeled "bull" before being tested in the real drama of the ring. There, the fate of the flesh-and-blood bull is certain but the vivid sequence of events culminating in its death is violently unpredictable. The *torero* tossed and downed by the bull was shaken but unhurt and recovered to deal the final blow.

The zoom lens was ideal for photographing the fast-moving sequences of these fights. My own position among the spectators did not allow me to move about so that with a lens of fixed focal length the size of the image in the frame would have changed constantly as the bull and the *toreros* moved backwards and forwards across the arena. By using a lens with an adjustable focal length I could keep the image at a relatively constant size as I photographed rapidly changing sequences.

Pentax, Vivitar 70-210 mm, Kodachrome 64.

Portraits in natural light

Natural light changes endlessly with location, time of day and variations of weather throughout the seasons. The photographer cannot control it in the way he can the lighting conditions in the studio but utilizing its varied range, from harsh glare to the subtle effects of soft directional light, is one of the most stimulating and exciting aspects of photography.

In child portraiture, the photographer aims to capture the characteristic physical appearance of his model while at the same time revealing personality and mood. If the portrait is of a group, the prime aim will be to capture the relationship between the members. Using bright natural light,

indoors or in the open, provides a good opportunity to capture individual expression and gesture, and the distinctive personality of a child or the character of a group. The photographer can often work informally and with great freedom while the subject is unaware of his presence. Even when they are aware of the camera, children will generally react naturally and without inhibitions to a sympathetic photographer.

The gentle diffused light of a slightly overcast day is particularly suitable for portraiture. It reveals a full range of tones and colours without creating harsh shadows. The photographer can move about his subject freely and shoot from

many angles while the model can be relaxe does not have to squint into strong light.

Diffused lighting has the disadvantage of i inating the subject and confusing detail wi discrimination. Light-coloured objects, in ticular, can be distractingly conspicuous carefully integrated in the picture or elimi by changing the angle of view.

Hard sunlight introduces problems of contrast but it can create powerfully mod images and allows the photographer to use sh as a way of eliminating unwanted clutter. As sections in this book demonstrate, all lig conditions can be used to advantage.

Soft directional lighting, my favourite light for photographing people, allows the photographer and his subjects to move around freely without distracting shadows and sudden changes in exposure. It is ideal light for recording the tones in light clothing or detail in shadow as in the picture of the girls below, or the delicate skin tones of children, as of the little girl opposite.

The contrast of sunlit and shadow areas provides a useful way of manipulating the composition as well as conveying different impressions of children. When photographed in shadow area, the little girl with her arm in plaster did not convey my previous impression of pride in her injury and the background of shrubs and windows was distracting and complicated. I then brought her forward a few steps so that she was in bright sunshine. Despite having to look into strong light, she seems very pleased with herself and, because of the very contrasty light, the background has become simplified by recording as shadow.

Backlighting has helped portray the sunny and happy mood of the girls watching a puppet show at a party. The combination of direct and reflected light has produced an interesting range of tones from black to white. I have exposed to give detail in the shadow area of the foreground children.

The transformations of colour brought about by changing qualities of light can be used to strengthen the impact of a portrait or to give it a particular character. Even the high blue sensitivity of colour film and the effects of colours cast by nearby objects and surfaces can be used to subtle effect.

Light in the doorway illuminates the figure but leaves the background sufficiently dark for the details not to be distracting. The blue cast has intensified the foreground colour and has contributed, as has the slightly soft focus, to the evocative atmosphere. The striking appearance of the girl—with goggles, swimsuit in disarray, damp hair and whimsical expression —has made an unusual but authentic portrait.
Pentax, 50 mm, 1/30, f2.8, Kodachrome 64.

Sunshine and shadow, only a few steps apart, have given strikingly different portraits of these boys. The change in the colour of the light has transformed the atmosphere and mood. The predominantly bluish light in the shadow gives an impression of shivering cold.
Pentax, 50 mm, 1/125, f5.6, Kodachrome 64.

Strong overhead light is usually considered not suitable for conventional portraits. Here it has created a warm and reassuring atmosphere and mysteriously masking shadows.
Pentax, 50 mm, 1/250, f8, Kodachrome 64.

Mixed lighting conditions

Good photographs can be taken in poor lighting conditions where a satisfactory result would seem impossible without using flash. Light from a 100 watt bulb, candle or even a single match can provide sufficient illumination for taking colour or black and white pictures. Indeed, the use of flash destroys the mood and feeling which are the essential strengths of such photographs, and creates an artificial atmosphere far removed from the original.

As well as allowing the photographer to capture realism and atmosphere, using existing light permits him to work more unobtrusively than would be possible with lamps or flash. Also there are situations where flash is unacceptable; babies, for example, can be alarmed by flash and young children rarely behave naturally when they are reminded of the photographer's presence by repeated flashes or over-bright artificial lighting.

Using fast film and lenses at wide aperture (f1.2–f2.8) in conjunction with slow shutter speeds makes it possible to work successfully under bad existing light conditions, although viewpoint and camera angle may be restricted. A mixture of natural light and weak artificial light can produce interesting colour results. The choice of film will also affect the colour balance of a photograph. Usually, the light that predominates should dictate the film you use but beautiful and dramatic effects can be produced by using, say, a tungsten film at sunset, which will turn reddish skies magenta.

Photograph with light from behind the camera illuminating the subject where possible, taking care not to mask the source. Evaluate the existing light and select a viewpoint, positioning the subject to take maximum advantage of the best-lit area. Look for such natural reflectors as light-coloured walls to reduce contrast, or use a white card reflector. People sitting or leaning against a wall can usually hold still for up to half a second.

Since slow shutter speeds are usually required under adverse lighting conditions, a tripod to eliminate camera shake is advantageous where circumstances permit its use. Otherwise the camera may be steadied by adopting a braced position against a wall, a table or a friend's back.

A sensitive light meter is helpful; the CdS type is preferable to the selenium meter, which reacts more slowly. Expose for medium shadow area where there is a single weak light source like 100 watt bulbs or oil lamps. The excessive contrast caused by localized areas of bright light can be turned to advantage, providing deliberately dramatic effects.

In poor light where detail is limited, the pose adopted by the subject should reveal some of that person's characteristics. Film cannot always record details you can see with your eye; for example, a room lit by the soft glow of a single lamp may look attractive but contrast will be so great that extra exposure for details will be required, which will also burn out excessive highlights. In minimal light, try uprating a fast film from, say, 400 ASA to 1200 ASA. This works best in soft, diffused light. Development time is increased correspondingly—cut off the first few frames and develop them first, adjusting the time for the remaining film according to the result.

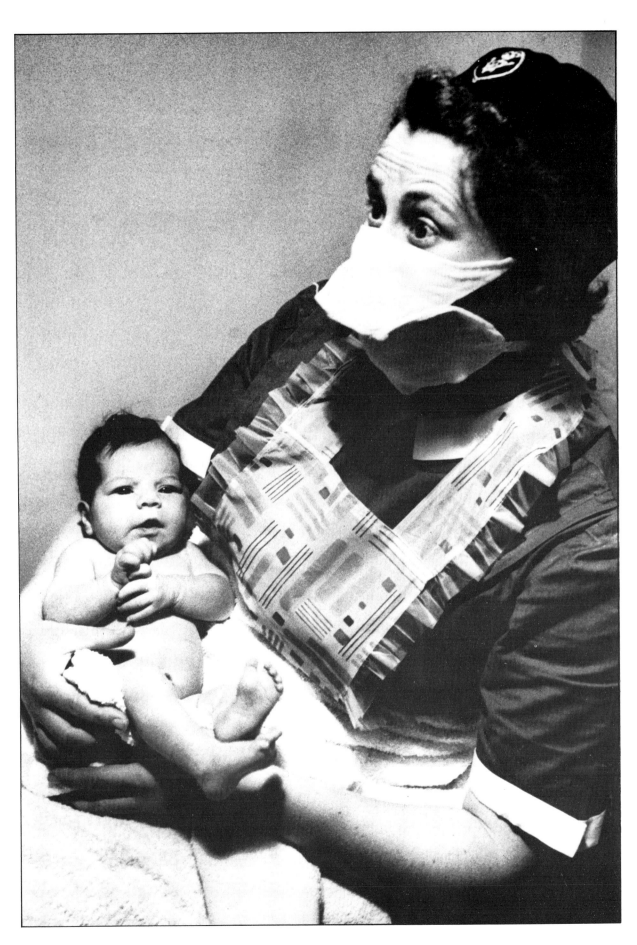

rst haircut (far
worth recording.
s are well lit,
few exposure
ms. I shot
st the light,
ing for the
wed face to
e the boy's
ssion.

e picture (left) I
ed the sparkler be
t arm's length
fireworks are
erous and extreme
ust be taken
using them to
atmospheric
es. The boy's
held the sparkler
foreground. I
lford HP4 film
30 at f5.6 here.

t hospital lights
ed me to photo-
the new-born
(centre) at 1/125
on a 100 mm lens
fast film.

epressing
sphere of this
tal waiting room
m) would have
lost with flash, so
a fast film and a
shutter speed
possible by the
ess of the sub-
Lighting was a
ard bulb —the arc
ws stresses the
onship of the
er and her sick
as he burrows
mfort into her
ective arms.

district nurse
t) is a vital part of
life, sweeping in
e control at times
ed. She bathed
changed this baby
was on her way
in ten minutes. I
1250 ASA film at
and f4 under a
att light. The
ground bleached
ut I was more
ested in the com-
ding eyes of the
and the secure
ntment of the
nestling against
mple bosom.

Modern cameras and fast films now make it possible to take black and white or colour photographs in light conditions that, until recently, would have defeated all but professionals.

By using existing light, the photographer can remain an inconspicuous observer, free to capture atmosphere and unselfconscious expression. Even the deterioration of colour in weak light or a colour cast can contribute to a truer and more interesting image than that created by additional lighting, which would show colour as if seen in daylight.

In mixed lighting conditions, the choice of colour film is normally determined by the kind of light that predominates: daylight film when daylight is the principal source of light, and tungsten film when artificial light predominates. The photographs below and on the opposite page were both taken, using daylight film, in a Portuguese restaurant. In that below, the proprietor's daughter has been caught reacting to her father's banter just as an outside door is opened letting daylight illuminate her face.

Composition and lighting focus attention on he mouth, which expresses so much life.
Pentax, 135 mm, 1/125, f3.5, Ektachrome 400.

The daylight fluorescent tube provides the ma source of illumination in the picture opposite. Though including the light has made it a powe element in the picture, attention is held down b the strong yellow of the ashtray and the intensi the girl's eyes.
Pentax, 50 mm, 1/30, f2, Ektachrome 400.

Studio lighting techniques

Photoflood tungsten lights arranged in a group can be used as the source of your "key" light. A screen of translucent white paper or cloth diffuses and softens the light.

An improvised studio provides controlled lighting conditions that greatly extend the photographer's scope. Children find a photographic session in a studio great fun but it is essential to have your lighting and equipment set up in advance as children soon become distracted or bored if they are kept waiting.

It is important to be able to experiment, so your lighting should be as easy as possible to vary. For most photographs, you will not need more than two lighting units. One will provide your main or "key" light, while the other, positioned on the other side of the subject, will provide "fill-in" light. Ideally, both lighting units should be mounted on lightweight, movable stands that are adjustable for height.

Tungsten lamps have the great advantage that you can see the lighting effect on the model while composing the picture and you can make exposure measurements with an ordinary light meter. But lamps are expensive and can distract your subjects with the glare and heat they produce. They also require relatively long exposures. Flash units are less obtrusive and their light is the same colour as daylight. Flash is also useful as a fill-in light source when existing light conditions are contrasty. However, it requires experience to judge the lighting effect they create. The required exposure can also be difficult to calculate when more than one flash is used, and you may need to buy a special flash meter.

The most useful type of reflector bowl is broad and shallow, providing a diffuse light. The light can be further softened by screening it with translucent paper on a white sheet or by bouncing it off a flat white reflector of cardboard, polystyrene, or crumpled aluminium foil. A white or grey wall or ceiling makes a useful reflector. Coloured surfaces, even furnishings, can produce colour casts. When you use the daylight available in your studio, you may need to soften it by pinning thin white paper or a sheet over the window. It is useful, too, if you are able to black out the studio completely because you can control the lighting effects more easily.

Usually there is enough "spill" available from your light sources to illuminate the background sufficiently, but remember that any unevenness in its brightness will be exaggerated by your film and may spoil the picture. A plain, light background with almost shadowless lighting creates a brightness of mood well suited to child portraits.

...ing for a formal portrait should never become a ...idding and daunting experience for your ...jects. By establishing a relaxed atmosphere, ...on found this brother and sister suggesting ...erent ways in which they could arrange ...mselves. A plain background and diffused ...iting have enabled me to take advantage of ...ir inventiveness and pleasure in what for them ...came a game.

...citing a natural response is an important part of ... photographer's task when taking portraits in ... studio. Your own confidence and a sympathetic ...tude will make it easy for a subject to react ...hout inhibition. Use a cable release and talk to ...ir subject while you are taking an exposure. In ...traying this teenage girl, I have taken care to ...w adequate modelling in her face and hair.

...essing up and careful grooming create a sense ... occasion to which many children react very ...sitively. This little girl was full of poise and ...nfidence so that I felt it was best to make the ...st of the period flavour in her dress and hair ...le. A chair provides a useful prop even when ...ir subject is not seated. To soften the formality ... these pictures I have experimented with a ...atively high angle of view.

...casual pose can be just as attractive in a studio ...ot as in a candid shot outdoors. These two ...ildren were intrigued by the photographer ...tting down to floor level. They have made a ...rong triangular shape that shows up forcefully ...ainst a plain background.

...oung children quickly lose their self-...nsciousness if given something to play with or ...me activity to be involved in. Lightweight boxes ...ovided the materials for a building game that ...pt this little girl amused during many sequences ... construction and demolition. A series of ...otographs treated as a montage makes an ...tractive alternative to a single shot.

Portraits are among the first photographs anyone takes. Family, relatives and friends are, after all, the most accessible and obliging subjects for candid photography. Formal portraiture involves an element of conscious posing but the same subjects are an ideal starting point. Despite the way it is described, a formal sitting should not be a staid and unexciting activity. If it is, there is a very good chance that the photographer will fail to gain the confidence of his sitter and without that there is little likelihood that the final result will be a sympathetic portrait. Particularly for photographs of children, using the home rather than the studio allows the photographer to establish an easy and relaxed atmosphere.

Family groups, as the one photographed here, offer intriguing possibilities for single portraits and for various combinations of family members. On this occasion, I chose to photograph in the family's own home, using a minimum of equipment: a camera fitted with a cable release and mounted on a tripod, and one flashlight fitted with a reflector as the only light source. I started with the whole family, and quickly established a relaxed mood. It is sometimes useful with a group such as this to break the ice by telling them a story or getting them to sing. In trying various combinations of the children, I was attracted by the idea of using the double chair as a central prop and built up a pattern of faces based on the twin sisters. Even with a group of this size, there is an enormous range of variations open to the photographer. While I wanted to convey the feeling of family in the group photographs, in the individual portraits I have exploited personal features—pretty hair, attractive hands and elegant profiles—and used furniture as props where it has helped the subject to pose.

69

Analysing the photographer's craft

Introduction

To capture the stages in the development of children from birth to adolescence is one of the most exciting and rewarding projects the photographer can undertake. I have chosen it as the theme for the analysis section of this book not only because of its intrinsic interest but also because it is a photographic project many parents begin with on the arrival of their first child. Your own family probably provides the material of the most absorbing and consistent interest. The pity is that so many projects are not carried through. I hope that my Photodiary will encourage you to sustain a project through to the point when your own children are grown up and that with guidance on the aesthetic and technical aspects you can turn your family album into an original portfolio.

I have not, however, thought exclusively in terms of the family photographer. My own Photodiary is not limited to a single family. Instead, I have aimed to convey the stages of growing up as they are experienced and observed in many different countries. Photographs of children, as photographs of any other subject, should and can have an interest that goes beyond our personal attachment to the subjects portrayed. One of the particularly attractive aspects of photographing children is that, despite vast differences of background, their expressions and gestures reveal our common humanity.

In the analysis pages, I look at the major compositional factors in photography: choosing the angle of view, exploiting shape and form, framing the picture, using tone and colour in composition and relating subject to background, all contributions to the success of a picture. I also look at the application of specialized techniques, such as panning to convey movement and daylight flash to freeze movement. I have also included other pages of analysis that lay the emphasis where I believe it properly belongs, that is, on the need to exploit the photographic potential of every situation, even if it means ignoring compositional and technical perfection. When photographing children, the first aim should always be to capture the characteristic but often fleeting expressions, moods and activities of children, wherever they may be.

71

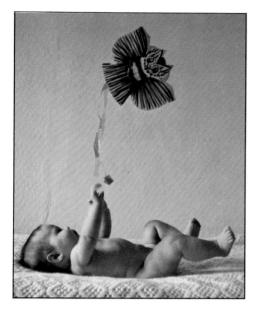

Babies and young children are highly
unpredictable subjects. Photographing them
successfully requires as much patience,
gentleness and understanding of children as it
does knowledge of photographic techniques. Good
results are most easily achieved when babies are
in warm, calm and familiar surroundings with
mother close to hand. Even in these conditions, a
photographic session should not last more than
fifteen minutes. Frequent short sessions are much
more productive than one that is long drawn out.
A well-lit position with uncomplicated background
avoids the use of flash, which can be disturbing to
very young children, and provides a setting without
distracting detail. By pre-setting the camera, the
photographer can concentrate on capturing
expression and gesture. When young babies are
to be photographed lying down, it is useful to fix
the camera on a tripod and to focus and frame so
that there is an allowance for slight movement of
the subject. Then, instead of peering through the
viewfinder, the photographer can look directly at
the child, communicating with him in a normal
manner, and take photographs at the appropriate
moment by means of a cable release.

A series of profile photographs taken over a
period of months or years provides an interesting
portfolio of pictures documenting development
from babyhood to childhood.
Pentax, 50 mm, 1/125, f8, Ektachrome 200.

By taking a simple approach to camera angle,
background and lighting, the photographer can
concentrate totally on shape and expression. Note
that the creased blanket helps convey a feeling of
warmth and movement.
Pentax, 50 mm, 1/125, f8, Ektachrome 200.

The anxious child is generally more cooperative in
the safety of his mother's arms. The relationship of
mother and child is strongly evident in this picture,
but positioning the mother in shadow has given
greater emphasis to the child.
Pentax, 50 mm, 1/125, f5.6, Ektachrome 200.

Varying the angle of view

By experimenting with the angle of view, the photographer can make the most of existing lighting conditions as well as controlling the composition and the way children are shown in relation to their surroundings.

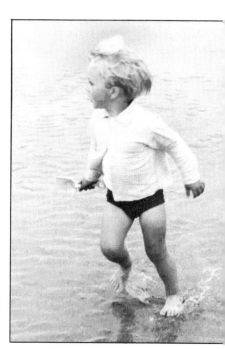

Parents photographing the family, just as much as professionals undertaking commissions, want their photographs of children to be interesting and varied. One of the most neglected ways of giving photographs variety—and one of the easiest to achieve—is to change the angle of view.

The inexperienced photographer tends to allow the camera and his own habits of posture to dictate the angle at which he photographs his subject. Armed with a single-lens reflex, he holds the camera at eye level and shoots down from a standing position. Such a viewpoint may produce very attractive results for some shots, but can often ruin others. Getting an interesting angle on children may mean crouching, sitting, lying on the ground, or standing on a chair while at the same time directing the camera upwards, downwards, to the left, to the right, or straight ahead.

Changing the angle of view not only enables the photographer to see children with a fresh eye and to capture the whole range of their activities and expression, but it also gives an important degree of flexibility in composing a picture. A relatively slight alteration of the angle may produce a very marked difference. For instance, it can transform a picture containing distracting detail and a cluttered background into one in which the subject, whether an individual or a group, is presented either in perfect harmony with its background or, alternatively, effectively isolated from it.

An interesting album includes pictures taken from many angles. The relatively flat angle used to photograph the boy on a beach (top left) has related him to a vast expanse of deserted sand. By taking from a higher level and looking down (top right), I have concentrated on the boy's shape and movement. In contrast to both of these photographs, the baby sitting on a beach (middle left) has been taken, using a Rolleiflex, at his own level. In capturing the child's pleasure at its first attempts to stand up (centre right), I have used a steep angle to contrast the light tones of the child with the dark background. Sometimes, however, it is impossible to eliminate all distracting detail. In photographing the girl in her classroom (bottom left), I used an angle that minimizes detail but suggests the setting. The controlled lighting conditions of the studio (bottom right) gave me the freedom to explore many angles and to wait for the right expression. When photographing a series, it is an advantage to have a single angle view and a plain background. For the photographs opposite I sat on a pair of steps in a well-lit, well-heated room and concentrated on capturing interesting shapes and expressions resulting when a contented baby was left to itself.

The appealing shapes and forms of children—delicate and vulnerable, or firm and robust—can say a great deal about their personalities. However, it is important to avoid striving so hard for compositional effect that the spontaneity and freshness of a child's behaviour or expression are destroyed.

Babies' clothing, which is often light in colour, is easily overexposed if photographed in bright light. Overexposure burns out the detail and destroys all the indicators of form, simply leaving the shape or outline. To capture the delicate tonal range and so fill in the form of the curious doll-like child photographed in a Peruvian village, I photographed in soft, shaded light, taking a reading from the child's clothes.
Pentax, 50 mm, 1/125, f8, Ektachrome 400.

The concentration of the little girl was captured using a medium-length tele-photo lens. Despite the unselfconsciousness of the subject, the picture contains elements of careful composition. The chair, clearly contained within a space, provides a frame for the child. Hat and chair are strongly related in shape, texture and colour and the daisy in her hand is a link with the flowered grass. The smooth body of the child and the delicacy of her form revealed in the weak evening light are subtly contrasted against the latticework of the chair.
Pentax, 135 mm, 1/125, f8, Ektachrome 64.

Shape and form in composition

The doll-like child was photographed in subtle lighting. I took a reading from the light-coloured clothing in order to capture the delicate tonal range.

Children and animals are often considered by professional photographers to be difficult subjects. They both give of their best over very short periods and yet, whether separately or in combination, they provide challenging and appealing subjects for all photographers. The boy and his cat together form a stable triangular shape but there is an element of tension.

Shape and form are two of the most important aspects of the physical character of an object, whether it is a person, something found in nature or something man-made. They are also two important components unifying the composition of a picture. Using them effectively can transform a snapshot into an interesting and original image. In child photography, however, the advantages of careful composition must always be weighed against the need to work quickly if you are to capture a fleeting expression or a momentous event, such as your child's first steps. The spirit of the photograph is always more important than the structure.

Shape is two-dimensional: it is an outline of an object without the content or depth. At its simplest and most dramatic, it can be a profile head in full silhouette. Lighting and camera viewpoint all play their part in using shape to give interest and structure to a picture.

The strongest shape can be that provided subject, as in the picture (right) where th provides an interesting triangular shape. Co ing the subject against a plain backgro against the light emphasizes shape and m more powerful in the composition. Altern the dominant shape can contain an image its form that contrasts both in shape and t The photograph of the little girl wearing hat (previous page) is held together by t bracing outline of the wicker chair.

Form is the descriptive element of an ob gives visual clues to its character and t solidity being conveyed by gradations i from light to dark. The contrast of lig shadow areas transforms the two-dimension three dimensions. Every lighting condition us form in a different way and it should accord with the form—soft light for delicat qualities, harsh light for drama.

The first steps are among the most important stages to capture if you are making a record of a child's development. The smooth arching body of this baby makes a dominant triangular shape contrasting with the carpet and cot.

Learning to crawl is an equally significant achievement. Here I have caught the precise moment of collapse after a triumphant few feet. A plain background sets off the sprawled shape of the child.

Though still a baby, this child was minding a stall in a market of the former Congolese capital, Elizabethville. I wanted to convey the child's vulnerability as well as the scale of his problem and so I took a close-up using a wide-angle lens so that the child appears as an anxious appendage to the bowl.

The strained pose of the South African boy, who had asked to have his photograph taken, reflects and emphasizes the uncertainty and tension in his face.

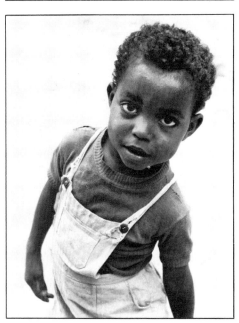

Every element recorded in a photograph contributes to its success or failure. The shape and positioning of children, their environment, and their clothes (especially the colours), and the quality of light are often as important as gestures and facial expressions. The vibrant colours frequently used in children's clothing are not always easy to handle but can be used to convey the boisterous energy and extrovert nature of some children or, by contrast, to highlight the meek demeanour of more timid children.

The Portuguese girl, photographed in her neat party dress, conveys, despite her self-consciousness, a strong feeling of repose. The blues in her dress supported by grey tones harmonize with the blue cast of the concrete floor and are a perfect foil for the delicate tones of her face.
Leicaflex, 50 mm, 1/60, f11, Ektachrome 64.

The vulnerability of the little Indonesian girl has been emphasized by the strong colour of her dress isolated in a subdued background. While the use of a long lens has slightly exaggerated the contrast in proportion, overcast conditions have helped create the impression of a harsh environment.
Pentax, 200 mm, 1/500, f5.6, Ektachrome 200.

Colour and tone in composition

Colour and harmony in the girl's clothing and background, and the uncomplicated composition have contributed to this powerful and sympathetic portrait.

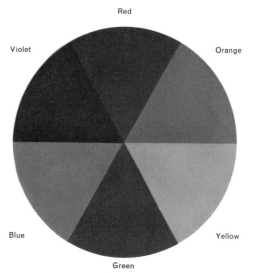

Red

Violet

Orange

Blue

Yellow

Green

The circle indicates the way in which colours register as tone when recorded by black and white film. In colour photography, you can use colour harmony and contrast to compose your pictures. In black and white photography, it is graduations of tone, shown here as a continuous shading from black to white, that provide the modelling and contrast which are such important elements in composition.

Though enthusiasts argue the respective merits of colour and black and white photography, each has its own qualities and strengths. You may prefer to record children in full colour but it is a serious mistake to think of black and white as a poor alternative.

In black and white photography, colour as well as shadow and light are reduced to a range of tones varying from black through to white. It is the variation of tone that gives objects their form. Harmonizing these tonal qualities in a picture is one of the most effective ways of achieving the illusion of volume and depth. The delicacy and lightness of high-key pictures—those in which light tones predominate—are often considered particularly suited for photographs of children. However, there are no infallible rules. Low-key pictures—ones in which dark tones predominate—can produce highly dramatic images. For most pictures the photographer will want to record a full range of tones in order to render the modelling with maximum subtlety. Exposure, development and printing are all factors that, combined with the ability to see a picture, finally create an interesting tonal balance.

In colour photography, the colour itself introduces a dominating compositional element to photography. Used with discrimination and understanding, colour can produce effects of great emotional as well as aesthetic power. What the photographer must consider is the way colours combine. Exploiting the harmony of closely related colours and hues can produce images of gentle subtlety. A random assembly of colour, on the other hand, produces confusing and jumbled images. However, using contrasting colours can be a way of adding emphasis to your subject or of giving drama to an action. Experiment using large areas of single colour, spots of brilliant colour, gentle monochromatic studies or the vibrant contrast of discordant colour.

To capture the indulgent satisfaction of this boy eating a luscious fruit, I wanted to record the modelling about his mouth with maximum clarity. Diffused light and fine grain film have allowed me to compose a picture consisting of a subtle range of middle tones.

The pleasure of mucking about in boats is powerfully evoked by this picture, which contains not only large areas of white and deep shadows but also a subtle range of middle tones. Though the light areas convey the luminosity of the water and the shadows give a feeling of depth and substance, it is the grey tones that link and balance them.

Photodiary/THE MISCHIEVOUS AGE

Playing areas, schools, homes and gardens, in fact most places where children behave spontaneously and energetically, usually have eye-catching backgrounds. These structural and decorative elements, often highly patterned, can be incorporated as integral parts of lively and intriguing pictures of children. When, however, patterned backgrounds are not carefully related to the activity or expression of children, the subject can be completely overwhelmed.

Interiors such as school gymnasia and dancing studios can be particularly difficult environments in which to photograph. However, rather than exclude the potentially distracting background of a gymnasium, I have used the rigid horizontal pattern of the wall bars as a contrast to the fragile form of the small girl.
Minolta, 50 mm, 1/60, f4, Ektachrome 200.

The expression and positioning of the little girl have linked her to the powerfully striped background in a way that no amount of manipulation could have achieved. Because my camera was pre-set, I was able to capture the instant when the strongly patterned background and subject were fully integrated without having to hesitate to make adjustments.
Pentax, 50 mm, 1/250, f8, Ektachrome 200.

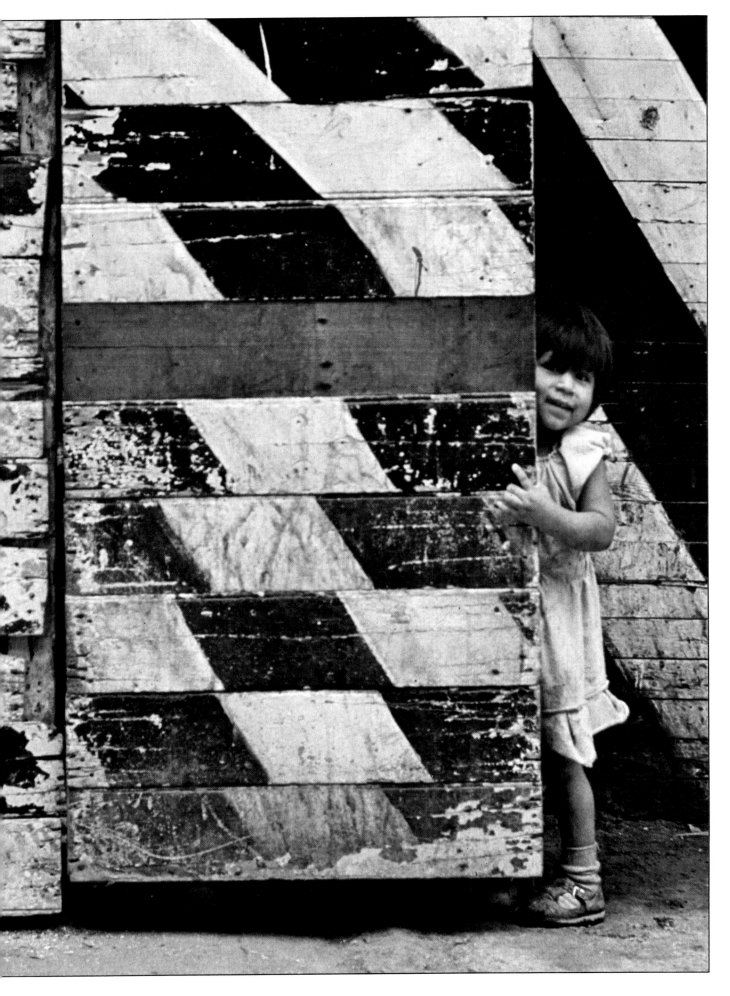

Background pattern in composition

Background pattern can add interest and vitality to your pictures of children provided it does not overwhelm the main subject.

Sharp or blurred, strong or receding, backgrounds are important because of the way they relate to the subject. The experienced photographer uses them, the amateur often finds they overwhelm his subjects. They are always there but often the eye is able to select or ignore them when taking the picture whereas the camera simply records them in all their detail and distraction. The photographer must train the eye to see potential problems in backgrounds because they are an integral part of the picture, they set the scene and they are vital when planning its construction.

As a general rule there should be one subject only and all other elements in the picture should be subordinate but supporting. If the background overpowers the intended subject the results will be muddled and disappointing.

Occasionally this rule can be broken, for example when your subject is arranged to merge into the background, its discovery giving the photograph an element of surprise. The picture of the burnt-out barn (above left, opposite page) is a clear illustration of how, in this case, foreground can be used as a camouflage.

Strong plain backgrounds can be used in stark contrast to emphasize a subject or mood. They isolate the subject's shape or heighten the detail. The little boy with the cardboard mask (right) is much more dramatic because he is against a plain background, and the two boys against the white building (far right) become silhouette shapes.

Backgrounds with a strong repetitive pattern are more difficult to control because they can often be too powerful and dominate the subject. Used carefully, though, a pattern can establish a motif, or bring order and rhythm to an otherwise static photograph. Patterns in black and white tend to add an abstract quality but in colour they create an emotional response of order and harmony.

Disordered pattern, that is pattern with a strong random element in it, can also have strength and unity, or it can be counter-productive and overwhelm the subject. Achieving a balance between the disordered background and the subject is usually a matter of proportion, and personal choice plays a vital part.

The waif-like fragility of this small girl is enhanced by the rough textured wall behind her. The linear pattern of the bricks also serves to emphasize her delicately patterned clothes.

The arrogant pose of this young boy is the strength of this picture. His face is hidden and the light background gives no further information but its bleakness complements the stance.

borately patterned background competes
e girl's shower cap but they are both forced
ubordinate rôle by the powerful and
ing nature of the girl's face. The picture
because the eye is drawn immediately to
e and is not diverted to the pattern.

ghting effect on the burnt-out barn in snow
ated an intriguing random pattern. It
ntarily hides the girl on a dappled horse
the structure but, after a closer look, the
verticals and horizontals form a clear
work for the subject.

A small boy potter in Sri Lanka sits surrounded by
his work. Both the beautiful shapes of the bowls in
the foreground and the dark silhouette of the ox in
the back are essential in revealing the boy's life-
style. In this picture the pots are as important as
the boy himself.

The cluttered façade of a service station provides
an excellent example of how random pattern
occurs in everyday life. Against this background
the two children and three dogs almost disappear
because both subjects and background have the
same degree of emphasis.

The strong shape of the building stands out clearly
within the picture area causing the two boys to
become silhouettes and blotting out the landscape. The contrasting black and white convey
the feeling of a hot bright day.

Photographers frequently fail to achieve a balance of subject and setting, children being reduced to insignificant dots in vast landscapes or, alternatively, the background being totally excluded. By choosing the appropriate lens—either to increase the field of view or to minimize it by enlarging the subject image—and by selecting the best camera angle, it is usually fairly simple to take pictures in which the subject and the background are fully integrated.

Children derive fun and excitement from repeating their activities, which gives the photographer time and opportunity to choose the best way to relate the subject to the background. Composition, lighting and colour have combined to relate these two energetic boys to the steep hillside they climbed again and again for the pleasure of running down.
Pentax, 90 mm, 1/250, f8, Kodachrome 64.

The flute player in the impressive Inca ruins at Cuzco, Peru, was photographed in the evening, when most tourists had gone and the light was fading to a warm glow. I positioned myself so as to isolate the boy's gentle but vertical shape against the hard outline of the most massive stones, thus achieving maximum contrast.
Pentax, 50 mm, 1/60, f16, Ektachrome 200.

Using strong backgrounds

Background and figures harmoniously related capture the spirit of a scene. Making the most of backgrounds can improve the composition of pictures as well as adding interesting information to your photographs of children.

Awareness of the physical setting is the first step in producing photographs that successfully relate subject to background. The beginner is so often intent on what he wants to see in the viewfinder that the background elements that can make or mar a photograph are completely neglected. In this way, faults are unconsciously included: there may be poles that seem to sprout from heads, splashes of colour that dominate the picture or a clutter of detail that distracts from the subject. It is even more likely that the novice will fail to see the positive features of a background that can be

used to enhance the technique of photograp[hing] children.

In photojournalism and documentary ph[oto]graphy, background is often used with pow[erful] effect to give an insight into widely varying s[ocial] and economic conditions. In family photogr[aphy] its purpose is not likely to be so serious and ye[t the] information a background supplies enlarges [the] value of these photographs as records of chil[dren] in a particular place at a particular time. A b[ack]ground can say a lot about the personalities [and] interests of children. It may be a way of ma[king]

The loneliness of this little Hebridean girl, photographed on the island of North Uist, is powerfully conveyed by the harsh landscape in the background. By using a shallow depth of field, I have kept the children in focus but lessened the impact of the background, which otherwise would have been too complicated and dominant. The subject is thrust forward but is, none the less, part of her environment.

The amusing pairing of boy and statue, photographed in a formal Italian garden, represents the kind of unposed photograph that is a happy reminder of holidays. A posed photograph, with the child simply standing beside the statue, might have been dull. The link between the child's eyes and the mysterious heavenward gaze of the statue has drawn the two together in the picture and introduced an element of fun.

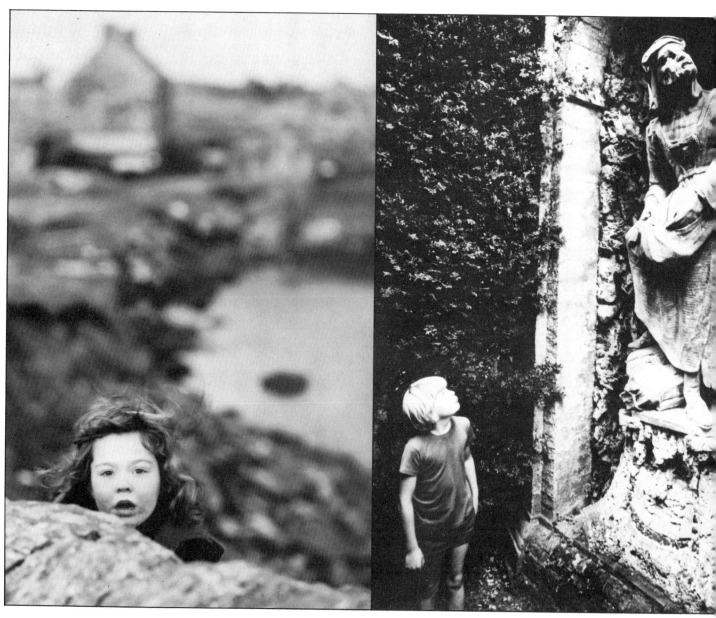

what activity children are engaged in or it
explain a particular grouping of people. It
so convey the special atmosphere of memor-
occasions.

ith holiday photographs, the prime motive
ften be to record children in relation to the
capes and monuments they are visiting as
ts. The photograph is a way of saying "I have
here", but you should always aim for more
just a blunt record. In taking travel photo-
s, it is frequently better to think of how the
ion of a child or group of children can enhance a picture of another subject. They may
simply provide a useful indication of scale, but
they can be used to bring life to an otherwise
static picture.

Whatever the importance of the information
conveyed by the background, it must be used with
discrimination to enhance the aesthetic value of a
picture. In any situation there is almost certainly
a variety of options that will produce interesting
pictures. The most obvious does not necessarily
produce the best photograph so it is always worth
trying more than one approach.

The choice of lens allows a considerable degree
of flexibility. Even with a standard lens, the
photographer has plenty of scope for altering the
relationship of subject to background by manipulating the aperture and so changing the depth of
field. A shallow depth of field can soften what
would otherwise be a dominating background and
yet allow it to convey all the information that is
needed. The photographer's greatest asset, however, will always be an alert eye and a willingness
to look at potential material from as many angles
as possible.

---

ey and girl, photographed in Indonesia, form
er amusing contrast, the old-man look of the
ey a foil for the vivacity and humour of the
ourists, children just as much as adults, want
ghtforward evidence of their trips to faraway
s. The discreet inclusion of appropriate
ground information, suggesting locality,
n and weather, provide keys to a bank of
y memories.

The plain dress and casual posture of the girl
contrast nicely with the elaborate decoration of a
Moroccan mosque. This is an example of a long
tradition in photography, bringing an element of
life into what would otherwise be a picture of
undiluted architectural detail. Though the background rather than the child is the subject, she
is an integrated element giving interest and a
sense of scale.

The uniformed girls in a convent school asked to be photographed and within a few minutes had formed themselves into a visually satisfying group. The apparently random way in which children arrange themselves coherently can be utilized in formal and informal situations. *Pentax, 28 mm, 1/125, f8, Ektachrome 64.*

A local band performing at a fête adopted this unconventional grouping when a storm forced them to shelter under a tree. Exposing for the shadow area under the tree has given a deceptively summery impression despite the overcast conditions. *Pentax, 35 mm, 1/125, f5.6, Ektachrome 200.*

The cluster of boys imprisoned in the bright blue window frame were easy victims when I suddenly turned my camera on them as they were watching me working. *Pentax, 50 mm, 1/125, f8, Ektachrome 64.*

Hands and feet as well as faces can express a great deal about individuals and groups. With this band of Portuguese children I was attracted by the variety of their footwear and their grubby bare feet. When they asked for their photograph to be taken, I focused on their faces and then unexpectedly turned the camera on their feet before they had a chance to move. *Pentax, 28 mm, 1/250, f8, Ektachrome 200.*

Analysing the photographer's craft

Photographing groups

A well-balanced arrangement of a large group is not always the result of the photographer positioning children individually.

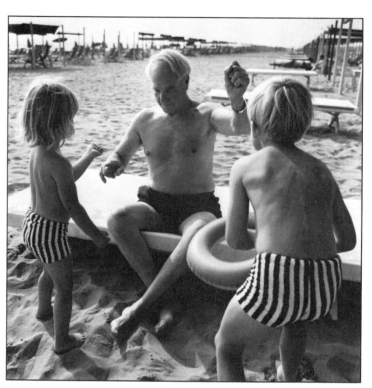

The easy relation spanning generat has been caught i moment of intens centration in a pri game. Even thoug have not included faces of the childr the image powerf conveys the mood the moment.

When photographing children in groups, it is important to convey what the function of the group is, as well as arranging them in a composition that expresses the purpose of the picture. It may be an interest in common, membership of a club or similar organization, or participation in a special occasion such as a wedding. In candid photography, the link may be a very short-lived one, a momentary and unstructured involvement in a shared activity.

In formal photographs of groups, clues to the link can be provided by uniforms and sporting trophies or musical instruments. Such emblems not only help to explain the nature of the group but also provide focal points. Arranging a group to best effect requires planning—although, as the key picture (above) shows, children will sometimes group themselves satisfactorily on their own account. You need a simple, uncluttered background and a way of organizing people so that the overall scheme is attractive and nobody is obscured. With a large group, children may need to be ranked according to height, perhaps in conjunction with seating. A wide-angle lens can be useful in photographing a large group but beware of distortion at the edges of the frame.

Bounced or reflected flash will give even lighting indoors. Diffused natural lighting outdoors will mean that children do not have to strain and squint while posing nor will they be hidden in dark shadows. Even in ideal conditions, you should always take enough photographs to allow for the many occasions when at least one of a group will blink or turn a head.

In candid photographs of groups, there is not the same need to portray each individual with equal emphasis. Instead, you want to choose a moment from a continuous event so that it sums up what is happening and makes clear the link between the children involved. The climax of an activity, the instant an action is completed, may be the most exciting and significant moment, but there are no rules. The anticipation of an event or the relaxed mood after accomplishment can be as revealing as a moment of tension or concentration.

Resist the temptation to treat all your subjects frontally or in profile. As the photograph of Henry Moore and two children (top left) shows, the feeling of a moment can be expressed just as powerfully by gesture and posture as by facial expression. As with all candid photography, you must be prepared to take advantage of opportunities when they come and your approach must be imaginative and flexible. Have your camera loaded with fast film and pre-set for speed and exposure.

The end of the line at a holiday camp beauty contest sho mixture of pride, bewilderment and anxious anticipatic at the moment of decision. Despite t varying reaction ar the linear arranger there is no mistakir the shared involve of the children.

Children pestering to be photographed are often taken aback when the camera is suddenly turned on them. When I reacted to the demands of these three boys, they measured their distance in a way that reflected their degree of confidence and their position within the group.

Father and sons, forming a tight-knit group on a motorcycle, were photographed from a moving car using a relatively slow shutter speed. What attracted me to the group was the contrast between the apparent danger and the confidence of the group, particularly the little boy steering.

Smiles of victory are just breaking out as this team of girls defeats a boys' team in a friendly and untutored tug-of-war. I have used a wide-angle lens so that I could get in close to catch the varying expressions and still take in the whole team.

The delicacy of a young boy's features is revealed in a reverse silhouette. An open doorway to a dark interior creates the black background, while daylight lights the boy's face naturally.
Minolta, 135 mm, 1/125, f8, Kodachrome 64.

Under her floppy hat the girl's smiling face is brightened by the reflection from the table. Her silhouette is contrasted against the garden background which I overexposed by two stops to reduce distracting detail.
Pentax, 50 mm, 1/250, f5.6, Ektachrome 64.

Low evening light created this Caribbean girl's spectacular shadow as she played. Speed was essential because a moment later the unique shape disappeared.
Pentax, 100 mm, 1/500, f8, Ektachrome 64.

The shape of the re tricycle was the in subject of this pict by chance the you stopped to watch i Her shadow and h matching colours helped unify the photograph and brought it to life. T result is a more sat image than of the t alone.
Pentax, 28 mm, 1/25 f8, Ektachrome 64.

Strong Portugues makes the group's sharply defined sh the most powerful of this picture. Fror directly overhead, figures themselves almost invisible.
Pentax, 100 mm, 1/5 f16, Ektachrome 64.

Silhouettes and shadows

A simple but strong image is created by the contrast between the dark background and the fine, light features of a young boy.

A young rider returns home at sunset. A low camera angle close into the horse exaggerates the shapes and distorts the head. The result is a dramatic profile against a placid sky.

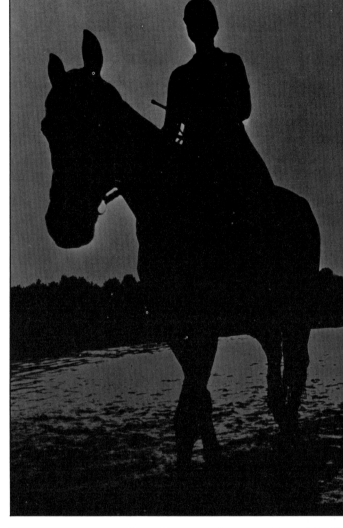

Silhouettes and shadows create sharply defined shapes and areas of darkness which help make dramatic pictures. They have a sparseness and an economy of detail that is at once attractive and strong. The simplest example of a silhouette can be seen at sunset when the sun sinks behind the trees on the horizon, their outlines becoming black against the light sky. Shadows produced by figures also create focal points as forceful as (and occasionally stronger than) the subject itself.

Used in portraits of children, the silhouette can sum up a character and expression as meaningfully as an ordinary photograph by the revealing profile of the head, or even simply of the nose, chin or mouth.

The easiest way to shoot a silhouette is to place the child against a bright natural light, such as a window or door. Expose for the background only in order to lose the detail on the child. If you are printing it yourself, increase the contrast by using a hard-grade paper. Indoors, or in a studio, set the unlit subject against a white background evenly lit with two or more spotlights. Outdoors, place the subject against a bright sky and take the photograph from a low camera angle. In both situations, expose for the light background.

A reverse silhouette (see page 96), where the subject's face is fully lit and the background is dark, is an alternative which will give you a strong profile while still revealing the features.

A semi-silhouette is a compromise between the opacity of the full silhouette and the detail of the reverse silhouette. The subject is set against a light background but a side-light or reflector gives some detail and form without destroying the pure shape.

Shadow silhouettes can provide a surprising element in impromptu photographs. The picture appears more three-dimensional because the flat shadow contrasts sharply with the continuous tonal element in the pictures. Shadows, such as those of the group (on the previous page) seen from above, offer a surreal aspect, seeming almost to have a life of their own. Whether they form the subject or support it, they should not be ignored, because they provide vital descriptive elements.

Shadows must be captured without hesitation because they are constantly changing according to the angle of the sun and the quality of the surface on which the shadows fall.

Silhouettes and shadows are a rich source of ideas with which to enliven standard portraits and candid photographs. By contrast, fine detail can be accentuated and greater prominence given to areas of the picture that in direct light would have lacked significance.

The mother and child with donkey in the Sinai Desert make a picture that has a great simplicity of line and a peaceful atmosphere. It was taken at a very low camera angle against the bright sky which emphasizes the silhouettes. The stark background accentuates the figures' isolation.

Simple silhouettes can be achieved by placing the child in front of a bright window in a darkened room and a frame of tracing paper between him and the camera. This diffuses any highlight detail from the background.

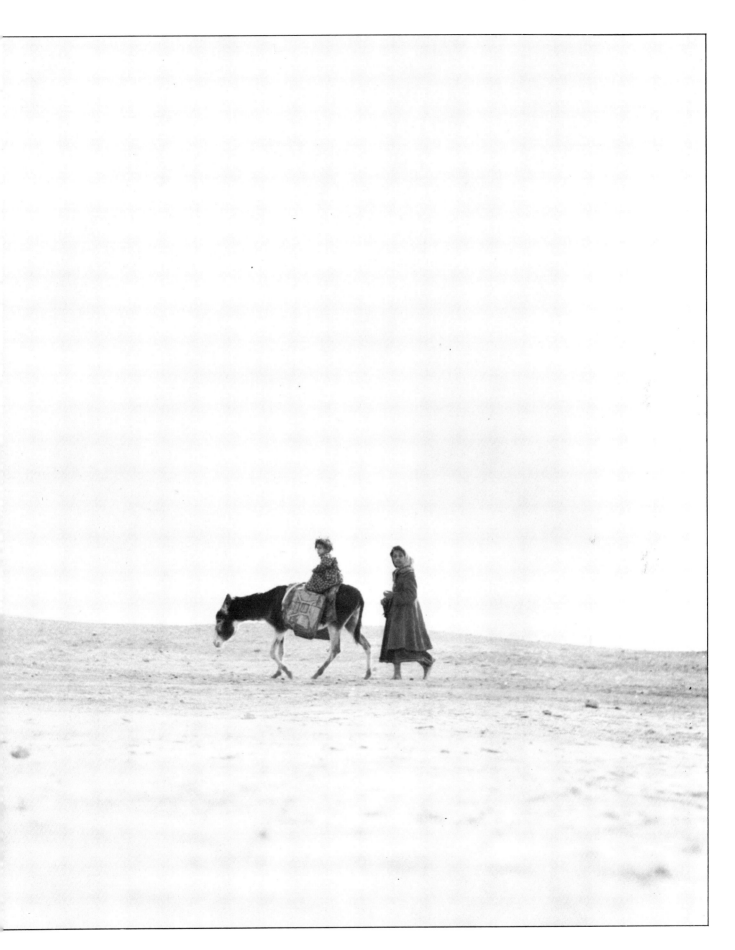

The jean-clad legs of the model's sister have provided a powerful and unusual frame for the girl dressed in a brilliant harlequin costume. This mobile frame, appropriately a single colour, allowed me to block out distracting peripheral highlights. At the same time, it has reinforced the shape of the subject and given the picture a sense of depth.
Pentax, 100 mm, 1/125, f5.6, Ektachrome 64.

Two children peering from the dark window of a creeper-covered building made me think of fledglings in a nest. To reinforce this idea, I deliberately included a large area of the façade and its wonderfully rich pattern of leaves. At the same time, I have taken care to omit other distracting features, such as drain-pipes and doors.
Pentax, 28 mm, 1/250, f8, Kodachrome 64.

Analysing the photographer's craft
Framing the image

An unorthodox frame such as the one formed by legs spread apart echoes the triangular shape of the seated girl.

The door, flanked symmetrically by windows, trees and posts (below), frames the girl and her nanny within another frame formed by the foreground window.

The two boys are looking out of the picture (bottom) so intently that it needs the presence of their mother, framed in the window, to arrest our gaze and hold it on them.

The contrast of sky and building reflected in the window (right) is an integral and menacing part of the frame surrounding the grandmother and child.

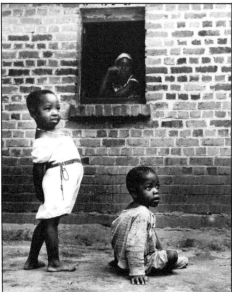

One of the most straightforward ways of giving interest and emphasis to your pictures is to frame the subject with subsidiary elements of the composition. Architectural features—such as archways, doorways and windows—are the most obvious, but still effective, shapes that can be used in this way. By including familiar architectural forms in photographs, their proportions can be seen in relation to, say, a child, and thus add information to the picture. As a foreground frame, they can be used to channel the view through to the subject beyond. Used in the background, their outlines can contain and focus attention on subject.

Architectural features are far from being only framing devices the photographer can and merely giving emphasis to the main subj not the only function a frame can perform simplifying pictures, the first step is to mini clutter and distracting detail in order to g clear view and understanding of the subject. object can form a frame to mask extraneous but a linking element that supports the su should be sought. The range of possible objec purpose is almost unlimited: foliage, rocks, s, buildings, statues or animals. A photogra- can easily make his own frame by cutting s in either plain or coloured paper. I have even a torn film carton, held a few centimetres in t of the lens, in order to mask distracting il.

s well as obscuring unwanted detail, framing ces can also fill in uninteresting foregrounds mpty skies with colour, tone and texture that rast with or complement the subject. Over-ging branches can, for instance, close in the

ping babies happy (below) may limit the angle pproach. I have made a virtue of necessity by g the cot against a dark setting as a frame.

air with a solid back (bottom) provides a very ul frame for photographs of young children. It unwanted detail at the same time as giving child support.

bonnet, combining with the collar to form a orative frame (right), sets off the face of a small d momentarily fascinated by the photographer.

subject and create an evocative atmosphere. Devices of this kind are useful for masking the sun when photographing into the light. They can dramatically increase the sense of depth by suggesting a succession of receding planes.

When using a frame, and often it will be in more than one way, combine its use with selective focusing. Although the subject should be in sharp focus, generally the frame will serve its purpose best if it suggests the haziness of peripheral vision. A shallow depth of field allows the subject to be sharp and prevents the frame from overwhelming

the picture. For correct exposure, take a reading for the main subject rather than a general one for the whole area. A foreground frame can be most effective by using the high contrast of a dark foreground, for example, looking through a dark archway to a gently lit subject.

Using a frame that supports the idea of the picture calls for imagination and a willingness to experiment with both the angle of view and different focal length lenses. Look at the photographs through this book to see what an important compositional device framing can be.

When composing a picture, one normally tries to contain the action or the spirit of the picture totally within the frame. However, there are many occasions when interesting pictures can be obtained by ignoring normal conventions. Their dynamism relies on what is implied rather than what is stated, or simply on the element of surprise.

The little girl caught at the window is an example of a simple incident which, none the less, has made an interesting picture. There is a rich colour harmony but also an element of tension as the child struggles, feet perilously far from the ground, to peer through heavy net curtains for a glimpse of the television set, which is in the room out of sight.
Leicaflex, 50 mm, 1/125, f5.6, Kodachrome 64.

The girl and dog, one running, the other alert, are both reacting to something outside the frame, something to which the photographer might have been expected to turn his camera. The exclusion of this element rather than diminishing the force of the picture has created its mysterious tension. Other elements in the composition have also helped to heighten this tension. These include the strong diagonals, which are anchored in the firmly delineated dog and lead to the blurred movement of the girl, the spectral shadows, and the balance and linkage of tone and colour.
Pentax, 28 mm, 1/30, f16, Ektachrome 64.

Experimenting with composition

The strong area of the window is an effective compositional balance to the child firmly positioned in the lower third of the frame. Our eyes follow those of the child as she gazes through the window into the room beyond. Our interest lies in the conjecture of what holds her interest.

Composition is the selection and organization of the elements of a picture into a cohesive whole that expresses the individual vision of the photographer. It enables him to relate visually his reactions to his subject, so that the viewer immediately sees the full significance of the picture. Line, shape, tone, colour, texture, pattern, perspective, scale and depth are all important elements of composition. Though there are formal rules borrowed from painting, for most photographers composition is largely a matter of intuition, combined with a sense of balance and harmony.

Try to keep things simple: in general, choose a single, dominant subject in each picture and make the rest of the picture relate to and support this theme. The eye should go immediately to the main subject, then roam easily over the whole picture area—but always being led gently back to the central image. Too much going on in a picture usually results in the eye being bombarded with visual information, and the viewer becomes first confused and then bored. A well-composed picture makes a strong initial impact and then offers the opportunity to study the supportive effects.

Balance—the visual harmony between elements of shape, line, tone and colour—is important. This need not imply a symmetrical arrangement: on the contrary, a useful guide (the so-called "Rule of Thirds") is to divide the picture horizontally and vertically into equal thirds and to position the key elements of the picture on or at the intersection of these divisions. This can be used to balance out the relationship between foreground, middle distance and background.

Depth relates the subject to its setting. It defines the spatial relationship between foreground and background using perspective. This is seen mainly through *linear perspective* (convergence of lines receding into the distance), *aerial perspective* (colour and tone fading into the distant atmospheric haze), *diminishing scale* (objects looking smaller when further away) and *overlapping forms* (one object partially obscuring another behind it). Scale indicates the comparative size and importance of objects. Areas of mass need to be balanced against one another, since they give the overall weight or bias of a picture. Where the photographer stands in relation to his subject and the lighting on it will also have a strong effect on composition. If time permits, walk round your subject, viewing it through the viewfinder from all possible angles, to find the best viewpoint. Do not be afraid to take many shots of the same subject from different positions. Sometimes great patience is needed to wait for just the right expression or approach.

Composition in thirds has positioned the boy learning to swim firmly in the lower part of the picture. It is at once obvious what the main subject is, but the rest of the shot is still of strong relevance: the earnest expression of the boy links closely with the watchful eye of his teacher, and the receding continuous tone leads us gradually from the foreground towards the background figure.

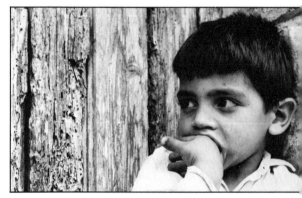

The child's face, and thus the focus of our attention, is to one side of the frame. But see how the direction of the boy's glance, and the curve of his thumb, automatically lead us to the left. The vertical lines make our eyes rove over the rough boards, contrasting their texture with the smoothness of the boy's skin until we are compulsively drawn back to the eyes once again.

ar perspective, the
nishing lines and
es converging in
distance, highlights
positioning of this
n a long corridor.
tunnel effect and
highly symmetrical
ngement concen-
e our attention on
exclusively.

ial perspective
tes foreground to
dle distance and
kground. Other
rs give an illusion
epth through
inishing size. The
hers are sand-
ned between fore-
und and dominant
ustrial background.

camera angle
s strength to this
of a boy with his
dump truck,
phasizing its power
strength. Shooting
nto the shadow
makes the toy look
e substantial. The
of trees helps this
tical thrust. In this
d of picture we are
ering the child's
gination and treat-
toys as if they were
size. If we tilt the
nera, we give an
sion of speed to a
tionary go-cart.
pth and the distance
ered are suggested
he track's curve.

hlights and deep
dows contrast
ongly in this picture,
ding the image
izontally into
ghly equal areas of
eground, middle
tance and back-
ound, giving an
hosphere of repose
n idyllic setting.
e boy and his bicycle
positioned off
ntre, their shapes
hlighted against an
stract background.
e foreground
adow leads the eye
the tree trunk into
dark foliage of the
ckground, framing
e cyclist.

Holiday pictures should capture the relaxed mood and spontaneity of children, their sense of freedom and the excitement of new places. Have your camera with you at all times so that you do not miss vital moments: when it is always there, children ignore it and behave quite naturally. The perfect photograph, in terms of technique and composition, may be difficult to take on a crowded beach bathed in brilliant sunshine but what will make your photographs worthwhile is the way they capture the liveliness of your own children and of other children about you. Be careful not to underexpose faces. Reflected light from sand and sea can give deceptively high exposure readings. Remember that seawater and sand are potentially harmful to your camera. Take every reasonable precaution to protect your equipment and make sure it is adequately insured in case of loss or theft.

Cropping for impact

A candid shot taken on a beach becomes a more intimate portrait when cropped to remove an unwanted person in the background. It reveals the sinuous quality of the girl's body which contrasts with her childish pose.

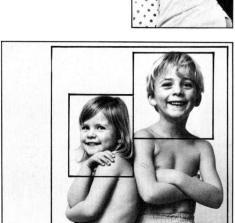

A photograph can be composed for better effe in many ways. Here, a portrait of a mother and young baby is shown cropped in landscape an portrait formats. Both are successful because distracting background and lower half of the mother have been removed and the eye goes straight to the facial expressions of the two subjects.

When taking a photograph, the photographer has many considerations before pressing the shutter. One of the most important of these is composition: also shape, form, texture, colour and tone, as well as the overall harmony, contrast, balance and rhythm. The experienced photographer tries to develop an "eye" for the requirements that will enable him to compose and take shots instantly because, in general, it is best to compose pictures within the frame formed by the viewfinder. Some photographers find that using the hands to frame the shot before taking it (see illustration above) helps rule out unnecessary clutter. Occasionally, however, there just is not time to consider every aspect, or to change the lens or position and, in these situations, the photographer can resort to cropping the picture afterwards in the darkroom.

Cropping in this sense means selecting only part of a negative to enlarge for the final picture. In order to give yourself more freedom to do this, when taking the photograph allow a good area of background around the subject.

Whether a picture is cropped closer before it is taken or afterwards, cropping helps simplify a picture by cutting out distracting detail; it allows greater importance to be given to the subject and causes the eye to be directed to the focal point. Always think before taking any picture—have I included any unnecessary elements?

Since life does not always arrange itself to fit the camera's format (even when there is time to compose the shot), cropping gives you a second chance to perfect or change the emphasis of a picture. It helps to improve the candid shot taken because the mood, light or subject was suddenly right, even though the entire composition was imperfect. Perhaps it was marred by an unwanted item in the background or distracting highlights.

If your picture does need cropping after you have taken it, place L-shaped frames (illustrated above) to block off the unwanted areas on the contact print (or the full-sized print). Draw in the area required on the print and use it as a guide for the enlargement. Enlarge the new image to the desired size and shape.

When applied successfully, cropping is a useful tool of the photographer but it is no substitute for careful preparation and insight.

A good group portrait with all subjects responding is a rare thing where children are concerned. This is where cropping is particularly useful and, as seen right, smaller pictures can intensify the focus of attention on the child as an individual. Alternatively, if you find that your picture is fundamentally sound but that it has distracting areas of clothing, colour or limb positions, these can also be cropped out to good effect.

Horse-riding is a passion with many English teenage girls. Here, the speed of the horse's gallop is captured by a fast exposure and emphasized by the way the picture has been cropped. The long narrow shape suggests energetic forward motion and high velocity.

Most photographers compose the potential shot through the viewfinder. Alternatively, they hold their hands (far left) in front of their eyes as a viewfinder. This helps remove superfluous detail and reveals any imbalances. After you have taken the photograph, you can further crop it by using two right-angled black L-shapes (left) to mask off the unwanted areas on the contact print before enlarging the negative.

A beautiful child in Sri Lanka was photographed with a normal lens from a distance (left), in order not to disturb her wistful expression. By going in closer or changing lenses I would probably have disturbed the child and missed this shot, so a solution was to take it and then to crop out the unnecessary background afterwards. The result (above) is, in fact, a much more dramatic and sensitive image.

A distant group of small girls (above) seems lost in the long empty alleyway and their characters are impossible to detect. By making a closer crop (below) the attractive lines of cobblestones still take the eye into the picture but now the girls' smiling faces bring life into it. We can also see that the middle girl is being taught to roller-skate. The picture could also have been cropped to make a vertical, or portrait shape, which would have emphasized the narrow alleyway.

111

atic moods and
ions of children,
h show so clearly
mmediately in
faces, change
laughter to tears
ack again with
ishing rapidity.
otographing
ren, capturing a
ficant moment is
matters, even
it means that a
re is not quite
ct technically or
ositionally. To
d the shifting play
rsonality and
gs in the features
ildren, the pho-
pher has to shoot
instant. With a
ter speed of 1/125
ore you will be able
tch fleeting ex-
sions provided you
lert enough to
the opportunity
it comes. For
shots, I prefer to
lens in the 90—
mm range as it
s you can fill the
without crowd-
he subject and
out getting a dis-
d image. Using a
dard lens can
that you are
ding disconcert-
close to the sub-
and possibly
ng your own
low onto your
el. However, there
o inflexible rules—
oy at the bottom
of the selection
was taken at close
e with a 28 mm
-angle. As this
tion shows, these
dren are rarely self-
scious, even when
ing at the camera.

ting for smiles and
hter should not
e you to miss the
lay of other
tions, such as an
onsuming if
ting moment of
appiness. The little
(right) is totally
rbed in expressing
despair, yet a
nent later he was
hing happily. The
rait was taken
de using light from
ndow.
ax, 100 mm, 1/125,
Ektachrome 64.

Capturing the moment

The most powerful photographs of children record the play of expression and emotion on their faces. Be prepared to shoot at once when the right moment comes—it may not be repeated.

Children are made for candid photography, displaying a fascinating range of emotions that makes superb subject matter. A single session—or even sequence—can produce a full range of human emotion, from pathos to rage. Although children frequently play to the camera, the novelty can soon fade and they will return to normal behaviour. If they do not, stand further back and change to a long-focus lens. Alternatively, take a series and leave a few exposures in reserve. Announce that you have finished and resume shooting the moment they relax.

Children are natural performers and may your efforts to obtain spontaneous reactions. this to advantage—their posturing can pro interesting results. Even the opposite reacti shyness, sometimes encountered when the tographer is a stranger, can produce captiv photographs. As a last resort bribery, fla cajolery or cunning may be necessary.

Setting up an ideal situation in which chi are encouraged to participate in a specified ac is a rewarding way of getting lively and intere pictures. After supplying the impetus, give

A noisy game of cards was in progress while I was reading in the garden. The commotion made concentration impossible. It was easier to photograph it than fight it, so I took this sequence recording the children's total involvement in the activity, and the changing pattern of triumph and disappointment. Such sequences should be picture stories. It is unnecessary for each shot to feature a dramatic moment—the calmer moments have their place in a faithful record of the activity as a whole.

Children love painting and there is endless potential in turning them loose with paints and blank paper. The contrast of attitudes is striking—the girl on the left is stretching to the limit, the boy has lost interest and the other girl expresses lively curiosity at what is happening around her.

"Boy with cello" c be a formal portrai but I was intereste the subject's almo dream-like absorpt in the music. Natur light from the side picks out the stron shape of the instru and highlights the and hands.

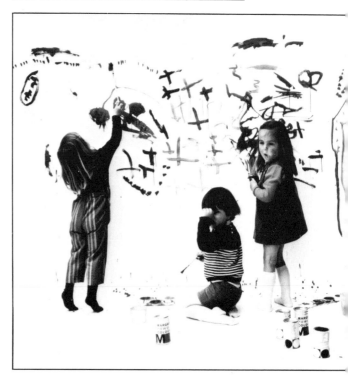

l freedom and wait until they become absorbed ore starting to shoot. Never force children to operate—their natural instincts are usually icient. I prefer photographs of children to be vity-based, illustrating their relationship to the vity and reason for being involved. I continue oting until I feel the potential of the situation xhausted.

Where children are the subject, the photogra-r requires quick reflexes and rarely has the nce to re-set camera controls. Children move y fast, so it is important to be prepared. Diffused lighting allows maximum flexibility, and exposure may be pre-set. Weak sun or light overcast sky are ideal for outdoor work, while indoor sessions work best with an overall light source. Even when children wander about, the photographer does not need to make constant exposure adjustment.

Taking account of prevailing light conditions, use a film that allows shutter speeds of at least 1/125, preferably 1/250 seconds. This enables you to catch spontaneous movement and quick re-actions. It is often impossible to use fast shutter speeds inside, in which case flash is preferable to bright studio lighting, which can take some time to set up and may make children self-conscious. Remember, though, that young babies can be frightened by flash.

I often use a wide aperture setting to create a shallow depth of field, bringing the subject in to sharp focus and blurring conflicting background that would otherwise detract from the effect. I also carry a second camera, pre-set for the conditions, in case I run out of film at a crucial moment. There is nothing more annoying than missing such a moment—once passed, it is gone forever.

ool work obviously rests the girl on the ht. I emphasized her mplete concentra- by bringing her face sharp focus but pping right down to give a narrow th of field. The ction of a specific a of interest is nforced by the ple tonal effect of extraneous content.

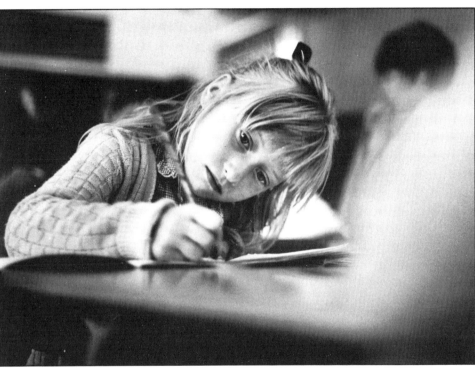

The music lesson (below left) was awkward to expose, with the main subject area between two windows. However, I like the relationship of figures, surroundings and activity, which provide an integrated picture. The child's emotions cannot be judged, but her teacher's reaction is sufficient clue.

Another music lesson —this time Sri Lankan style—has a strong tri-angular composition. The position of the teacher at the apex is stressed by the low angle of view. The drummer is performing confidently. The teacher watches the boy on the right, who is much less sure of his performance.

Children mimicking the behaviour and gestures of adults provide the photographer with many opportunities for interesting photographs. It is essential to work quickly because manly stance and defiant gesture, for example, can change in an instant to a light-hearted response. Always include sufficient background to make clear the purpose of a child's action and to set the scene of the activity.

The self-confident, firm stance of the boy seems to depend on the sense of security the rifle has given him. Whatever the cow might do, the boy is in complete control. His position, forming a cross at the centre of an exceptionally three-dimensional picture, reinforces his formidable posture. The sense of depth has been created by the road, which draws the eye in along the interrupted line, and the succession of horizontals formed by the cow

and the shadows created by strong side-lightin The right-hand line echoes the central line of th road and seems like another barrier to the movement of the cow.
Pentax, 50 mm, 1/500, f5.6, Kodachrome 64.

The guard at the château gates is a little French boy brandishing a rifle to block our way in. He helds the rifle in a man-like way but at the same he childishly hides behind it, using it to cover his eyes. The colourful clothing completes the pression of a sentry warning us not to step from the dark shadow of the gateway into the bright ht of the courtyard.
caflex, 50 mm, 1/500, f5.6, Kodachrome 64.

Pre-setting the camera

The dynamic quality of this photograph depends on the precise positioning of boy and cow, which I was able to capture by recognizing the potential of the situation and acting quickly.

Capturing unusual moments may be partly chance, but for the good photographer it becomes instinctive to be in the right place at the right time. It is also a matter of awareness, of guessing how the situation is likely to develop, and being ready to use the camera with a minimum of adjustment in order to capture spontaneous actions that appeal. Having the camera pre-set and loaded with fast film will provide maximum flexibility. Automatic cameras can be a help in rapidly changing conditions, but make allowances if shooting against the light, or pictures will be underexposed.

The girl on the clothes line was part of a group of children playing in a neighbour's garden, encouraging each other to more and more exciting and dangerous activities. When children are aware of the camera, as here, they are often spurred to extravagant and comic behaviour which, none the less, can be very revealing.

Regular weight checks for young babies take place in the butcher's shop in this remote Northumberland village. Since the closure of the chemist's shop, mothers with babies to weigh queue with shoppers buying meat. Forewarned, I came in inconspicuously and captured a bizarre scene, giving another meaning to "family butcher".

Photodiary/THE ENERGY OF CHILDREN

The vitality of children is often best expressed by including an element of movement in the subject. Panning (swinging the camera during exposure) creates background "speed lines", which increase the sense of motion and speed.

By vertically panning the camera, I was able to convey the movement of the boy on a trampoline. The artificial lighting in the gymnasium limited available shutter speeds and apertures. *Pentax, 50 mm, 1/15, f3.5, Ektachrome 200.*

The liveliness of the Peruvian boy is effectively conveyed by the contrast of blurred and sharply defined areas. A faster shutter speed would have frozen all movement on the boy. *Pentax, 50 mm, 1/60, f16, Ektachrome 200.*

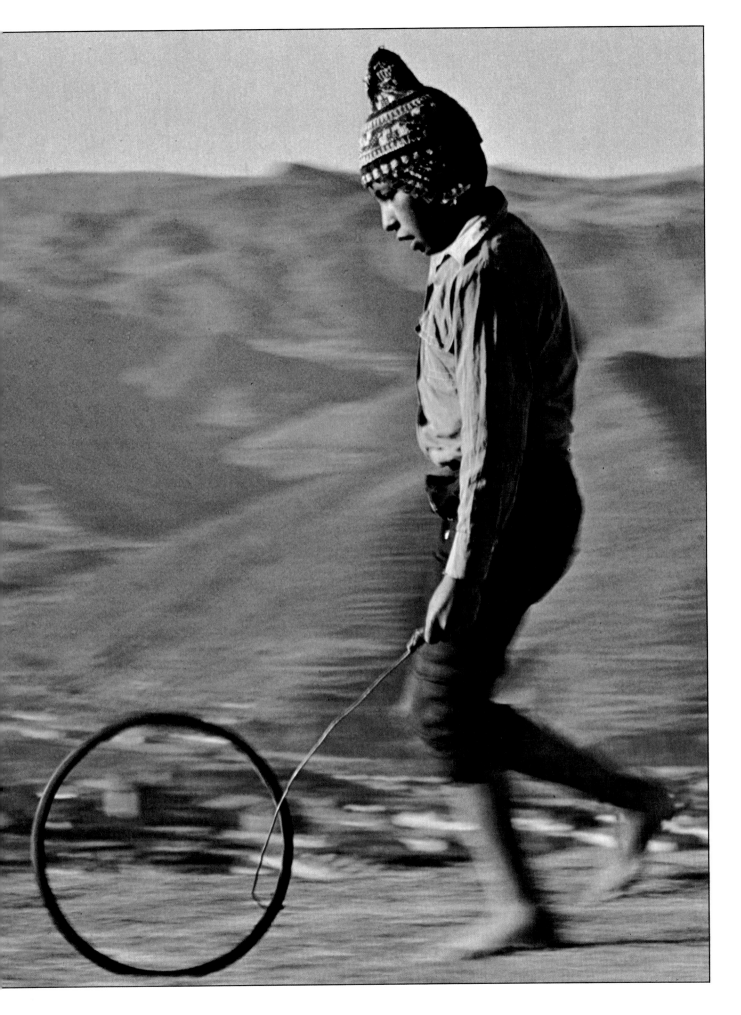

The use of panning

Panning movement should follow the subject. I used a vertical pan for the child bouncing on a trampoline.

The dancer's motion was arrested by a shutter speed of 1/1000. The low angle exaggerates the size and importance of the dancer in relation to the room, and her graceful mid-air position is sufficient statement of her movement.

The technique of stopping a fast-moving su by the use of fast shutter speeds enables the tographer to record movement accurately in a the human eye cannot. While a subject froze mid-action can communicate the nature of m ment in various ways, the result is sometimes appointing. Moving subjects tend to lose the s of motion against the sharply defined details static background, relying totally on the posi and character of the subject to express movem This technique can work—as shown by the ph graph of the dancer (left)—but there are o ways of communicating the idea of movem and vitality.

By following a moving object with the car —panning in a horizontal arc in line with the ject's movement, releasing the shutter at chosen moment and continuing to pan smoo —the result will be a clear image of the sub against a blurred background. While the prin is straightforward, each shot will be governe circumstances—the subject's speed, path, dist from the camera and desired result.

Panning offers endless scope for the creatio striking photographs. Consider the purpose of action you are recording and decide if there moment that sums it up: a child at the apex c swing, for example. In such a picture the cha element always plays a part—it could be the a of the swing, the contrasting background or

A firm stance is required for successful panning. Set the exposure and focus on the chosen point in advance. Frame the moving subject as soon as possible and pan with a smooth movement, turning the body from the waist up to follow the subject. Release the shutter as the subject passes and continue to pan without interrupting the smooth movement.

A garden swing alw attracts children and makes an ideal subj for the use of pannin technique. In this ca it enabled me to reco the expression of the boy in sharp detail. T capture the spirit of swing's movement I panned in an arc tha followed its progress I kept the viewfinder firmly on the boy's fa The setting was 1/30 f16. This resulted in speed lines on the jumper of the small b in the foreground which add to the sense of movement.

The boy on a bike wa a good subject for th most usual type of pa ning shot, where the subject moves in a straight line across t photographer. I adopted a crouching position to emphasiz the height of the fror wheel from the grour and used a shutter speed of 1/125. The background was ide for a panning shot, w a change of contrast from light to dark.

ment of the child's body that makes it suc-
[...]. In such photographs, the chance element
[...] plays a part. The unforeseen is an exciting
[...] of photography. It is always worth ex-
[...]enting with the effects of slight blur,
[...]ally if the subject is rather pedestrian. In
[...]osing, a speeding cyclist may be more effec-
[...] one side of the picture area, emphasizing the
[...]g of fast movement over a given distance.
[...]elationship of subject and background must
[...]e considered—a lone runner can be panned
[...]st a large landscape to stress the solitary
[...]e of the activity, or shot in close-up to convey
[...]ysical effort involved. By selecting a slow
[...]r speed, the subject itself may be slightly
[...]ed, becoming an identifiably defined but un-
[...]d image that effectively communicates the
[...]ment of the moment, such as a hurdler at
[...]retch or a soccer player making a tackle.
[...]e direction of a panning shot should follow
[...]bject. The most usual pan is where the sub-
[...] moving across the photographer's viewpoint
[...]traight path. Vertical panning was necessary
[...]he child on a trampoline. Action can be re-
[...]ed by angling the shot so the subject's
[...]ty becomes unbalanced. Following the sub-
[...]hrough the viewfinder, the subject-to-lens
[...]ce will be changing all the time. Either stop
[...] to give increased depth of field or focus in
[...]ce on the spot where you feel it is most likely

the moving subject will be photographed. The
closer you are to a moving subject the faster the
shutter speed needed to reveal detail.

The blurred speed lines that emphasize movements in panning shots, giving them much of their
character, are caused by the moving camera draw-
ing highlights across shadows or vice versa. It is
therefore necessary to select a background with
contrast between light and dark areas to take maximum advantage of the possibilities. The slower the
pan, the longer the speed lines will be. A standard
lens is good for panning shots because it is easy to
handle. If a longer lens is necessary to cover a
sports event, consider using a tripod with panning
tilt head for smoother action.

Panning is one technique where the SLR is not
ideal, because the subject is invisible through the
viewfinder at the crucial moment of exposure. For
this reason I often use a direct-view camera when
panning. It is possible to get an auxiliary frame
finder for attachment to the accessory shoe of
an SLR, which helps overcome the problem by
allowing the subject to remain in view throughout
the operation. The TLR is awkward for panning
use—it has the disconcerting characteristic of re-
versing the subject's direction of travel in the
viewfinder, and waist-level panning is difficult.
However, many TLR cameras are fitted with a
sports finder which folds out of the hood, permitting direct framing and eye-level use.

The shutter speed will vary with the speed and
distance of the subject. As a guide, most movement can be panned at 1/15 or 1/30 to give a sharp
subject image and blurred background. Fast-
moving objects like cars may require 1/60 or
1/125, and it is possible to achieve a blurred background at 1/250 if the panning movement is fast
enough. Use the slowest speed possible—it is
desirable to use a small aperture to give greater
depth of field, making it easier to frame and hold
the subject.

It is quite possible to "stage" a panning shot if
you have control over the subject. Children are
usually willing to cooperate enthusiastically on
such a project. The action may be repeated over
and over again, allowing you to plan the shot and
try alternative angles of view and shutter speeds.
It is possible to experiment in the same way with
certain subjects that cannot be controlled—for
example, a race where contestants lap the track
several times. An advanced use of panning is the
communication of a sense of movement through
the creation of pattern alone. This is particularly
effective in colour photography where colours
and hues can be merged together or altered to
produce beautiful colour effects.

Mastery of panning takes time and practice, but
the effort is worth while. Once the basic technique
is properly understood, panning may be used to
create many exciting pictures.

Electronic flash has effectively caught the movement of the girl striding towards me. By using a slow shutter speed and swinging the camera through an arc during exposure, I produced an interesting background, radial lines carrying highlights into shadow. *Pentax, 50 mm, 1/15, f22, Ektachrome 200.*

The surrealistic in of the boy was ach using electronic fl. on an automatic camera operating fast shutter speed metering for the fo ground. The dart h immobilized again darkened sky, the writing on the dart clearly visible. *Vivitar, 24 mm, auto matic, Ektachrome*

Flash for speed

Speed lines in the background add to the sense of movement, while electronic flash has effectively frozen the girl in mid-stride.

A dramatic silhouette (below) was the result when I used 1/500 at f8 on a dull day—the speed required to freeze all movement.

The correct exposure to capture detail in these conditions was 1/125 at f2. This would not have stopped the action, so I used daylight flash at f11 and exposed for the highlight of the boy's face. The speed of the flash froze the dart, and revealed details of features clearly.

In the failing light would have been i possible to freeze skateboarder's ra motion without fla I selected my spot the camera and awaited the right moment. In the ph graph below, I und exposed the sky, n an effective dark b ground for the fig

The possibilities of recording movement can be extended by the use of daylight flash. In light conditions that do not permit the setting of a shutter speed fast enough to freeze movement, electronic flash (which at short distances may produce a flash with a duration of 1/300 to 1/10,000 of a second or less) can be used. The duration of the flash rather than shutter speed determines exposure and the movement arrested.

When photographing children in action, flash can serve a dual purpose. It stops movement and, when shooting against the light, helps fill in detail of the subject that might otherwise be lost and result in a silhouette effect. The use of flash on moving subjects in daylight, in conjunction with slow shutter speeds, produces a combination of detail and blurring that adds to the sense of movement. This is caused by the recording of small amounts of ambient light.

Synchronized electronic flash may also be used to create unusual results when photographing certain types of moving subject—high-speed machinery, water from a hose, a bag of flour hitting the ground, a girl at full gallop on a horse—with a clarity that cannot be achieved by the human eye, which records the composite movement rather than its individual elements.

It is possible to achieve good results in these areas with a simple camera, providing it is possible to synchronize for electronic flash. Bulb flash, with a duration of about 1/50 second, is less effective, taking longer to reach maximum brightness and dying away less quickly.

The combination of flash and daylight works well in colour—electronic flash has the same colour temperature as daylight, and discrepancies are minimal. For portrait work—against a bright sky, for example, where flash is required to fill in detail on the face—care must be taken to avoid "red-eye" caused by flash in line with the lens being reflected back from the eyes. The darker the room, the more pronounced this effect will be, as the subject's pupils will become dilated. To avoid this, use the flash from an angle rather than in line with the lens axis, or bounce the light onto the subject from a reflector card. Bounced flash, although requiring more exposure due to the increased distance the light must travel, helps avoid the loss of form and texture that is evident with hard, direct lighting.

Because of the brief duration of electronic flash, it is difficult to judge what will happen when the light falls on the subject. In the studio an instant camera equipped with flash is often used to test exposure, but this is rarely possible with outdoor subjects. To calculate correct exposure for a photograph combining flash and daylight, work out the aperture setting for flash alone, based on the dis-

tance of the subject from the camera. Redu aperture half a stop or more to allow for th light. Then, with the aperture fixed, meter shutter speed to expose for the background ensures that the subject (the area covered b flash) will not record too brightly in relati the rest of the picture.

A simple method of calculating flash ex is to use the guide number advised by the facturer of your flash unit for the rating of th used. Divide the flash-to-subject distance in appropriate guide number to determine t quired f-stop. This applies both to feet and n For fast-moving subjects like the skatebo shown above right, the exposure should b determined from your chosen position s you are ready to shoot instantly.

The use of electronic flash to record mov is an effective technique in conditions that v otherwise preclude successful shooting, ticularly in poor daylight where the use shutter speed fast enough to freeze the would result in serious underexposure an of essential detail.

As correct exposure under these varyin cumstances is difficult to calculate precisel perience is the best guide. It is therefore practising the technique in order to attain sistently good results.

mid-air drama
ow) is enhanced by
shadow caused by
n, which helps to
arate the skate-
rder from the back-
und. Here the
dow is a vital part
e photograph, but
anted shadows
spoil flash shots
ess care is taken to
d them.

Electronic flashguns have a calculator disc
enabling you to determine the aperture settings
required for various distances. You set the film
rating, turn the disc to the distance of the subject
from the light source and read off the correct
f-stop. The flash guide numbers are worked out
on the basis of the inverse square law. This is a
mathematical formula for establishing the
increase or decrease in the intensity of light falling
on a surface as the distance between the light
source and the surface alters. As the diagram
(right) shows, if distance from source is doubled,
the intensity of light on a surface is quartered.

Memorable pictures of children can capture the atmosphere and excitement of thunderstorms, fog, rain and snow. Modern films are capable of recording many of the special light qualities characteristic of different types of weather, ranging from the intense colour of storm clouds to the delicate tones of mist and the luminosity of snow.

A rainstorm has left the black tarmac wet. It reflects the sky and, therefore, seems light grey. Reflected light from water lying on a surface can often be exploited in this way to transform what would otherwise be an uninteresting background. Because the jacket is saturated, it has absorbed more light than when dry and so its colour is strengthened. The wet hair, of course, also appears darker.
Minolta, 50 mm, 1/250, f5.6, Ektachrome 64.

Bright, frosty morning light has vividly illuminated the bold colours of the girl's clothing, while capturing the subtle tones in her face and in the background. The vibrant red of the glove exaggerates the foreground while the blues of her other clothes appear to retreat. Blues and reds are beautifully blended in her chilled face, harmonizing with the intense colours of her garments.
Leicaflex, 90 mm, 1/250, f2.8, Ektachrome 64.

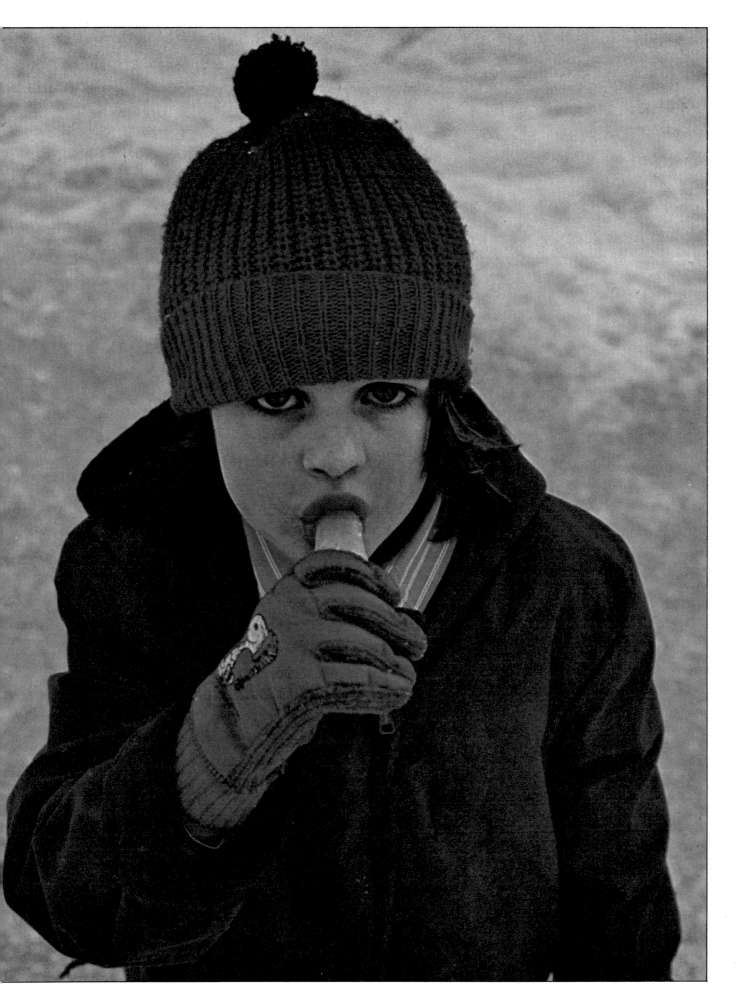

Photographing in adverse conditions

A frosty morning is encapsulated in this picture of a young girl sucking an icicle. Her subtle skin-tone is clearly illuminated by the bright morning light and enhanced by the bold colours of her clothes against a cold blue background.

Contrary to popular belief, bright sunny conditions are not always the best for taking photographs—some of the most interesting pictures have been created in unusual weather conditions.

Children love snow and are happy to play in it for a long time, which gives the photographer ample time to catch a candid picture. They are also usually uninhibited in snow because of the exciting opportunities it offers. A snow scene can be delicate and picturesque or dramatic and full of leaden tones if taken in such heavily overcast conditions as just after a snowstorm. Essentially, a snow scene is a monochromatic situation, so the intense colour of a child's clothing can give a picture considerable impact if balanced correctly against the background.

Photographers often have problems w taking an exposure reading of snow, so it is a g idea to bracket the exposure, taking one or frames on each side of the "correct" expos half a stop apart. If using a hand-held meter, ta reflected light reading holding the meter clos the subject's face or, if the child is some dist away, use your own hand to avoid underexpo of the flesh tones.

Although uncomfortable, rain is useful to photographer because it transforms colours creates shiny surfaces on previously unexcit subjects. The possibility of spectacular re usually makes the effort of photographing in rain worth while. If it begins to rain hea protect the camera with a plastic bag with a

he lens and keep on a filter (preferably 81A) to
ent rain getting on the lens. With stormy skies,
ose for the highlights to capture the dramatic
ground.

he atmospheric effects that are produced by
and fog, which are often such attractive
ures of landscape photographs, can also con-
ute to successful photographs of children. In
y and misty conditions, light is diffused by
sture in the air, producing very gentle model-
. Expose for the highlights if you want to
rd mist or fog—it can provide a useful back-
nd, blotting out or softening detail that might
rwise make the composition confused.

When travelling abroad you may encounter
more extreme weather and atmospheric

conditions. Protect your camera and films from
severe heat and cold, sand and dust and water
(especially sea-water).

Sand and dust are serious problems to cameras.
They jam the mechanics, scratch the lens and wear
the lens threads. Before going to an extremely
dusty location, wrap the camera in a plastic bag
with a hole for the lens and one for a hand. Seal
with tape around the edges. Protect the lens with
a filter. If any dust does get on the lens, do not
attempt to wipe it off—blow it off with a puffer
before cleaning with a lens tissue.

In a tropical environment, the enemy is moisture. High humidity encourages rust, which ruins
the accuracy of the lens iris movements and shutter
gear trains. Moisture also leads to the formation of

moulds both in the camera and on the film.
Transparencies are extremely susceptible to moisture and should be stored in special containers.
When not using them, keep your camera and films
in sealed plastic bags with several packets of silica
gel, then seal these hermetically in a camera case.
The gel will need drying out from time to time by
placing the packets in a warm oven.

In very hot countries, do not leave your camera
unprotected in the sun because it may melt the
cement holding the lens elements in place, causing
permanent damage. If possible, keep the camera in
a silver coloured case to reflect the sun. Store film
(exposed and unexposed) in a metal case with a
thick polystyrene inner case and try not to open it
in the heat of the day.

uiet churchyard by
Thames caught my
because of the
resting triangular
pes created by the
ding paths and the
rch itself. The threat
summer storm in
evening sky, which
phasized by using a
filter, provided a
p counterpoint to
peaceful landscape
the two strolling
ngsters.

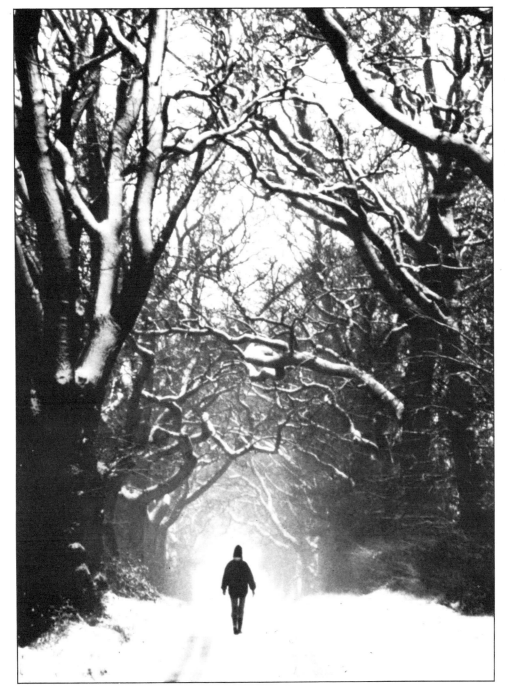

A sudden snowstorm
has transformed a
bleak and forbidding
Suffolk lane into a
beautiful winter scene.
The delicate tracery of
the branches topped
with snow form a
vaulted arch into the
distance. As the girl
walks down the lane
she is dwarfed by the
trees and yet she forms
the focus point, giving
scale to the compo-
sition. To avoid flare
from the bright fore-
ground snow the
exposure was based on
an average meter read-
ing from the shadow of
the trees and the high-
lights of the snow.

The warm light of early morning and of evening provide exceptionally evocative atmospheres for photography. Relatively mundane objects often take on a new life and figures become integral parts of their settings. The reddish-orange haze subtly transforms colours and plays tricks with perspective. Sudden shafts of light can bring drama, contrasting brilliant colour and shadow. It is worth getting up early or staying until dusk to catch not only the quality of light but also the sometimes unexpected activity of children before and after their daily routines.

The Moroccan children finishing a day's work were photographed a few seconds after the sun had set. They and the landscape are bathed in an after-glow, which has intensified the oranges and reds while creating an atmosphere of warmth and calm. The combination of evening light and the use of a long lens has flattened perspective so that the landscape behind the truck looks like a backcloth.
Pentax, 200 mm, 1/125, f5.6, Ektachrome 200.

The dramatic lighting on the Peruvian children returning home was caught by anticipating the precise moment the shaft of light would fall on their brilliant costumes. The striking contrast between intense colour and the sombre shadow of their forms is set against a strongly modelled landscape floating mysteriously in the background.
Pentax, 135 mm, 1/60, f5.6, Ektachrome 200.

Analysing the photographer's craft
The changes of natural light

The evening light in Morocco after sunset casts a warm yellow glow over the landscape. This diffuses the colours of the children's clothes and skin tones, and has the effect of subduing shadow areas and highlights alike.

The success of a great many photographs is governed by the light in which they are taken. In the studio or at home this can be dictated by the photographer using artificial light but in the open the photographer must depend on available natural light and be able to recognize its favourable qualities. Sometimes this will mean waiting for the appropriate time of day to get just the right lighting conditions.

The time of day has a great effect on the kind of light there is. In the morning, when the sun is near the horizon, red light is predominant because the blue waves are filtered out by dust particles suspended in the air.

If there is little cloud, dawn produces a pure light that is excellent for photography and certainly worth getting up for. Sunrise causes the light to "warm up", to gain more red tones. Speed is essential at this time because the light chang quickly. As the sun rises through the mornin; sunlight becomes brighter and less favourabl though until about 10 o'clock it is still clean good and the shadows are sharply defined bu completely black.

Midday light is hard, less red and directly c head. Although daylight colour film is bala to reproduce colours most accurately under r noon daylight, on the whole it is not a good for photography. When taking portraits the st light creates ugly shadows under eyes, noses chins and causes children to screw up their Avoid this time, if possible, or prevent these p lems by using flash or a reflector to fill in shadows. Better still, move your subject partial shade and expose for the face, not fo. sunny background.

n the late afternoon, the light again becomes
e suitable; it is low, warm (which is very good
skin tones) and it casts long cross-lights over
andscape. On hot sunny days there may be a
siderable haze in the background. Use an ultra-
et or 81A filter if you wish to penetrate it. The
it gets, the longer and more blue the shadows
ome. In mid-winter, of course, the afternoon
ry short and the light fails rapidly.
unsets are often colourful and exciting as
grounds but you need to be at the right spot
cord them because the light changes rapidly.
best to take a tripod because long exposures
be necessary.
Dusk can be a beautiful time; the light is dif-
d, the colours muted and there is a stillness
ch, if captured, can create tremendous atmos-
re in a photograph.

Filters

The use of filters can appreciably improve a
photograph in certain conditions; the sort of
filter you use depends on whether you are
taking black and white or colour pictures.
Special effects filters, which can be used with
any film, are discussed on pages 146-7.

Filters used for black and white film lighten
their own colours and those colours in the same
area of the spectrum, and darken complementary
colours. The effect is to increase the contrast on
the negative. A yellow or orange filter darkens
the tone in a blue sky and separates it from the
clouds. A red filter turns blue sky almost black;
the clouds remain white.

Filters for colour photography (known as
correction and conversion filters) change the
colour temperature of the light reaching the
film by increasing their own colours and
blocking out complementary colours. This is
useful for balancing the colour temperature
of the light when it varies from that for which
the film is made.

The 81 series of filters is good for improving
skin tones; the 81B adds a rich, suntanned
effect. Filters 1A and 2A add a pink tone.

Filters can either be glass discs or thin
gelatin film. Glass ones last longer than gelatin
but gelatin filters are cheaper. Treat your filters
as carefully as your lenses: do not touch or wipe
them except (with glass only) with a clean lens
tissue.

Coloured filters reduce the amount of light
reaching the film so unless you have through-
the-lens metering you must allow for this.

eak and menacing
strial landscape
matched by the
stormy weather.
ncrease the con-
between the
ds and the sky, I
d a yellow filter.
picture's hori-
al lines are inter-
ed by the stiff
cal cooling stacks
chimneys. A feel-
of movement is
oduced in an other-
static landscape
e homeward-
nd schoolboy and
hasized by using a
shutter speed, so
the figure of the
is recorded as a
ht blur.

isty morning, with
sun breaking
ough provides the
ospheric conditions
his Thames-side
ket match. The
all light gives a
used tonal range.
reflections of the
er station link the
kground to the
ground. In this
, the environment
armonized with the
vity of the boys.

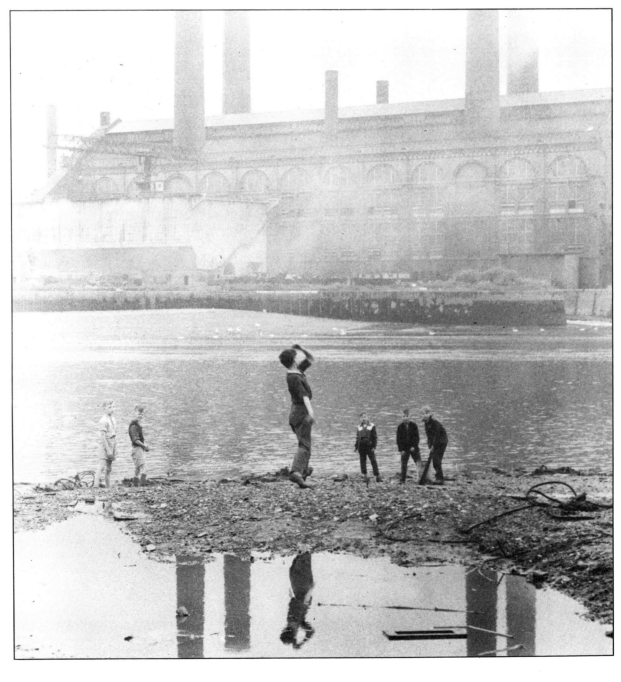

Organized sporting and physical activities provide firm disciplines for the exuberant energy of teenagers. Intense concentration on practising skills excludes self-consciousness. This concentration and the frequent repetition of movements, particularly in the dance studio and gymnasium, provide the keen photographer with wonderful opportunities to record the grace and agility of adolescents.

Natural lighting conditions, even in interiors with obtrusive backgrounds or furniture, can be turned to advantage in capturing the true atmosphere of a situation. In this front-lit photograph of a rehearsal, I have used the way the light falls off to exaggerate the perspective and to emphasize the relationship of the four girls. *Pentax, 35 mm, 1/125, f5.6, Ektachrome 400.*

Backlighting in the ballet studio has provided a luminous background against which to show the elegance and lightness of the dancer. I took a reading by standing with my back to the window to get an approximate value for the area in which the girl was standing and then opened the aperture one more stop so as to give detail in the shadow area. *Pentax, 35 mm, 1/250, f8, Ektachrome 400.*

The effects of backlighting

Backlighting is one of the most effective ways of conveying a sense of lightness and grace in subjects as well as being wonderfully evocative of a sunlit atmosphere.

The sunny atmosp of this scene reinfo the pleasure and excitement the little girl shows at being swung down the ste by her parents. As as conveying the impression of sun-f space, backlighting simplified the imag the steps reducing pattern of highlight and shadows.

The high spirits of t children enjoying a party in a beautiful summery garden ar wonderfully convey in this photograph t includes their danc shadows. Whicheve way I photographec this was a complica subject. The most interesting picture could find at groun level involved shoot against the light an using a wide-angle

The results of backlighting are well worth the problems caused by the contrast between highlights and shadow areas. On cameras that have manual controls, or automatics with override, effects will differ greatly if exposed for highlight, for shadow, or for an average of the two. Automatic cameras without override respond to high-intensity light and can cause underexposure.

If photographing towards light, use a lens hood and avoid shooting straight into the sun. Strong sunlight passing directly through the lens causes secondary images (halation effect) or flaring (a diaphragm image, as in the photograph below). However, the sun masked behind clouds, trees or buildings can produce impressive effects.

Long shadows indicate that the boy and cows (far left) were photographed in the evening, when backlighting has nearly reduced the shapes to silhouettes. The deliberate elimination of detail concentrates attention on the action.

The great contrast (left) of the glaring light behind and deep shadow in front has added a dynamic quality to the picture of a girl running. I have exposed to get some detail in the figure.

Rim-lighting can be very evocative of the fun and pleasure of outdoor living (below). The figures of children on a pole have been picked out against a cool, shady background.

The half-seen face of an adolescent girl, partially obscured by a veil, has produced a powerfully mysterious image. Despite the pattern of the mesh, the elegant structure of this girl's face is well defined. In order to give sufficient detail I have allowed for a half stop extra exposure than the light reading from the surface mesh. Any partially transparent material can be used to create interesting variations on more conventional portraits.
Leicaflex, 90 mm, 1/125, f8-f11, Ektachrome 64.

A telephone booth, bearing its crude message of love, is like a capsule enclosing the girl absorbed in her intimate conversation. The reflecting glass suggests an element of secrecy but allows us to see enough of the three-dimensional space to contrast with the bright red surface of the outside world.
Pentax, 50 mm, 1/125, f8, Ektachrome 64.

Reflections and distortions

Reflections on the window create an intimate atmosphere in which the girl feels unobserved. The glass also softens her image slightly and is a contrast to the hard red surround.

A great deal of the photographer's skill lies in being able to eliminate the problems of unwanted flare, reflection and lens distortion. Most modern cameras, with their coated lenses, fine optical glasses and filters, have been developed to minimize these difficulties. However, the creative photographer often uses these shortcomings to advantage, producing unusual effects and exciting photographs. Mirrors, water or any polished surface can reflect the image with varying degrees of distortion, and, when used imaginatively, enhance the subject.

Try using reflections when taking a formal portrait of a child. Set your subject either next to one mirror for a simultaneous front and side view, or between two mirrors at a right angle to each other for an infinity of reflections, a kaleidoscope of images. Experiment with different lighting techniques to make the result more dramatic.

When photographing a reflection in a shiny surface or in water, photograph the reflection and leave out the original. The image will be much softer and sometimes quite distorted so that you may not be able to identify the subject but you will have created a fantasy picture.

The fragmentary images between the subject and photographer caused by reflections on transparent surfaces can introduce an air of mystery. The young girl and her grandmother (below right) are not quite in our dimension; they are at once imprisoned and yet sheltered behind the window. The camera is almost intruding upon their privacy.

Photographing children through a window adds a touch of realism; it sets the scene. A window suggests that the children have not been posed or prettied and the spontaneity of the photograph is emphasized. The picture of the children seen through the car windscreen (far right, bottom), is a vivid example.

A polarizing filter can be used to remove superfluous reflections but you may find that your photographs have lost some drama and interest in the process.

A penetrating study of the girl's wistful face is achieved when she is placed next to a mirror. Diffused light is provided from a window which, reflecting off the mirror, gently lightens the shadowed area.

An unguarded moment has been captured between a girl and her grandmother. Their closeness seems to be reinforced by the framework of the window and reflections on the panes prevent the intrusion of the onlooker.

A polarizing filter blocks light reflected at an acute angle from a smooth, non-metallic surface such as polished glass, plastic or water. The filter is rotated until the reflected light disappears.

Minimizing reflections by using a polarizing filter (left) simplifies a picture but an image with the subject partially obscured by reflection can be more interesting.

These Singapore children were taken through the windscreen of a slowly-moving car. The windscreen does cause some distortion of image and colour but the result is acceptable. It is preferable, though, to shoot through an open window for most photographs.

Dressing up and making up are partly fun, partly
a serious matter of self-expression. Personal
surroundings add to a portrait by reflecting current
and often intense interests.
Leicaflex, 55 mm, 1/125, f6.3, Ektachrome 64.

The graffiti on the walls of a club room or the
paraphernalia of a bedroom evocatively record
teenage interests and exuberance.
Pentax 6x7, 105 mm, 1/125, f8, Ektachrome 200.

Creating the atmosphere

The interests and pre-occupations of a teenage girl have been conveyed by framing her mirrored portrait with the clutter of her dressing table.

The emphasis in child photography is on capturing the reality of a situation: an expression, a gesture, an action related to a particular environment. The photographer usually attempts to record as faithfully as possible what he sees before him. But there are occasions when you will want to use your skills to enhance a mood, to create an atmosphere or feeling that is present largely in your own imagination. Such effects, though engineered rather than natural, can still look convincingly real in the final picture.

There are two ways of going about this. One is by the application of photographic technology in the form of filters, lenses, types of film, darkroom techniques and so on. The other is to rearrange the elements of the picture deliberately, to make the setting look the way you want it to look rather than the way it appears normally.

Wide-angle and telephoto lenses can be used, as we have seen, to change the normal optical vision of the eye. The grain of fast film can add texture, and use can be made of the individual colour characteristics of different types of film. Filters are especially useful. Soft-focus or diffusion filters reduce the harshness and highlights of the image, giving a romantic, misty effect, which can also be achieved by lightly smearing petroleum jelly onto a glass filter. Fog filters have a similar effect, gently merging the colours and tones. Starburst filters can be used to dramatic effect to break up strong light into star-shaped flares. Try using one on such subjects as street lamps at night or the sun's reflection on water. Unlike most of the filters used for colour correction, none of these special effects attachments requires a compensating exposure increase.

Try also the technique of panning to convey the excitement and vitality of action situations. Flash can also be used to freeze movement and suggest speed.

Even without using any specialist equipment, you can still modify images to suit your imagination. Careful composition can disguise the way a scene normally appears to the eye and alter its context. A patch of waste ground in the middle of a city can be made to look convincingly rural, or deliberate contrasting with the background can stress the essential character of a subject. The defiant stance of the girl opposite is emphasized by placing her in a staid, domestic setting which typifies the life-style she is rebelling against. Beware of making the overall effect seem too contrived: the elements of a picture should complement, not contradict, each other. Use special effects that are relevant, not for their own sake.

To capture or emphasize a particula[r] atmosphere the use o[f] filters is often necess-ary. A soft-focus filter diffuses highlights an[d] reduces hard edges. Here the trees are softened so they do n[o]t overpower the couple creating an impressio[n] of a romantic walk through a sunny glade[.] Use wide apertures; stopping the lens dow[n] will diminish the soft-focus effect.

An ultraviolet filter w[as] partially smeared wit[h] petroleum jelly to fra[me] two students. I chose this method rather tha[n] a soft-focus filter as I wanted to use a smal[l] aperture to get both students and back-ground sharply defined.

Using a 250 mm lens from a distance enabled me to captu[re] this moment of passi[on] fairly close up. I in-cluded enough back-ground to support th[e] romantic mood, thou[gh] the setting was, in fa[ct] a piece of waste grou[nd] full of rubbish in a cit[y.]

A new dress is alway[s] an occasion for a photographic sessio[n] I wanted to underlin[e] the young girl's as-sertion of indepen-dence as it was expressed in her clothes and make-u[p] I consciously made a[ ] rather formal pictur[e] placing her in contra[st] to her parents' pre-tentious suburban home.

The daredevil IMPS

Six or sixteen, the Imps have one thing in common—guts and determination to excel in the spectacular world of display riding

The wheels that make it all possible, and a very little Imp (left). The team on parade (below) show the precision and discipline that characterize their impressive display.

THREE YOUNG MASCOTS lead the way into the arena, signalling the start of forty minutes of skills and thrills performed by the Imps Motorcycle Display Team. The crowd marvels at the disciplined precision of the formation rides and pyramids; applauds the skill behind individual tricks; laughs at the comedy routines—and gasps as a gleaming motorcycle hurtles through a ring of fire or soars above a line of cars and bikes. It is a truly professional performance, yet the performers are all unpaid school children between the ages of six and sixteen.

The Imps were formed in 1974 as part of a highly successful East London adventure scheme known as the Hackney Adventure Holiday Project. This independent voluntary organization was founded thirteen years ago by ex-military policeman Roy Pratt, a Senior Education Welfare Officer. In his professional capacity, he works to help juvenile offenders, providing a vital link between parents, schools, police and other agencies interested in the welfare of individual offenders.

Creative outlets

He was convinced that many of the problems he tackled daily sprang from the poor environment and deprived social conditions of East London. The Adventure Project was an attempt to provide country holidays and activities for local children, and to offer creative outlets for energies that might otherwise have been frustrated, with destructive results.

An early project involved the restoration of two elderly BSA Bantams, which were used to teach motorcycle riding. It was an immensely successful activity. In June 1974, five boys and an adult instructor performed at a Project Open Day in London to show parents that the activity was properly controlled. This first display went down so well that it was decided to form a team.

Through the following winter, a small group of boys worked hard in all weathers learning to master their machines and put a small show together. The publicity that followed a press visit to the lonely Cotswold farm where they trained gave

149

The daredevil
IMPS

the young riders a boost, and the team began
make a name for itself. By the end of 1976
Imps had starred in numerous television p
grammes and appeared all over the United Ki
dom, thrilling millions of spectators who w
astonished that such young people could w
together to master the split-second timing, di
pline and advanced riding skills that went into
spectacular display.

Isn't it dangerous?

Now the team travels all over Britain, and
Europe. A large transporter carries the mot
cycles (supplied by Honda after the compan
Japanese President saw a film called *Children of*
World that featured one of the Imps) and pro
while an executive coach carries staff and rid
The team performs only at weekends and in sch
holidays and is always accompanied by vol
tary adult staff—two instructors, three matron
care for the children, two mechanics, a te
engineer and the display commentator.

Roy Pratt explains how the team is recruit
"We have an open recruitment policy. A
youngster from the London Borough of Hack
may write (with parental permission) and ask
join. We then run a tough residential course
which the prospective members don't even s
motorcycle. The course involves communal liv
and very tough physical activity—we make
secret of the fact that it is designed to dissuade th
from joining us, and this usually succeeds
reducing the numbers to the level needed to
the vacancies caused by the retirement of sen
team members at the ripe old age of sixteen. T
new members are then put into serious trainin

"We're often asked if the display is dangero
but we believe that in order for young people
develop into responsible citizens, at some stage
their lives they need to take part in excit
activities. It is not possible to have advent
without some risk, but with training the risk
be reduced to an acceptable level.

e **discipline** and
nusiasm that direct
ebullient energy of
East End London
s (far left) who are
ud members of the
s team come from
military policeman
Pratt (right). The
gramme of training
organizes and the
mitment he
nands produce
cision coordinated
mwork capable of
h superb displays
he mobile pyramid
low left).

The daredevil
IMPS

"Many retiring team members continue to help the team on a voluntary basis. They pass on the benefit of their experience, and well over 70 per cent of old boys go on to find employment in the motorcycle industry. Their training, discipline and skill prove to be real assets in later life."

The success of the Imps may be judged by the fact that many members had very poor school attendance records before joining the team, preferring the streets to the classroom. This ceased to be a problem when they joined the team.

The spirit and objectives of the Imps Motorcycle Display Team are perhaps best illustrated by a fact that Roy Pratt relates with a pride that is tinged with sadness: "There are large blocks of flats in this part of London where virtually all the children living there have some form of juvenile criminal record—all, that is, except the ones who have gone and joined a group such as ours. I think it is an indictment of our society that so many children get into trouble and go off the rails for want of a constructive outlet for their energy and drive."

Through the hoop for a fearless youngster (below). Whatever your point of view, the simultaneous shots of the display's climax (right) add up to a heart-stopping moment as the team's senior rider soars over two cars and ten bikes.

The daredevil
IMPS

Having become proficient at child photography, consider turning your skill to further advantage. There is steady demand from commercial picture agencies for good individual photographs of children, which they purchase outright or sell on your behalf. It is possible to sell complete series of pictures which tell a story. The local press and trade magazines are always on the lookout for good material, either single pictures or features. If the idea behind the feature is strong enough and the finished result of high technical quality with good visual impact, the top magazines would consider the material and—if it's good enough— publish it.

Even if you have no interest in selling work, there is satisfaction in creating a successful series of photographs, whether for exhibition purposes or to give the family album an added dimension. Whatever the objective, there are general rules that can be usefully applied to the creation of good feature material.

The idea

Find an idea that has a strong theme with suitable potential for varied photographs that complement and illustrate important ingredients of the story. There should be human interest and emotional appeal—humour, drama, achievement, triumph over the odds—or convey information that is new and interesting. Consider likely outlets and study them to get a feeling about the type of material they use. The local paper can serve as a good source of ideas with its coverage of news and forth-coming events. A brief news item often conceals a story worth following up in depth. The paper is unlikely to have a photographer at every forth-coming event. Children make excellent subject matter—they are naturally appealing and often become involved in activities that are in them-selves full of interest.

Planning

Careful planning is essential. When the idea is formulated, consider how it may best be illus-trated. This may mean shooting over a period of time. For example, you might decide to record preparations for Christmas at a children's home, starting two weeks before the big day and building up to that riotous party on Christmas afternoon. It may be necessary to obtain permission to shoot. Conditions may be difficult, requiring an assort-ment of film. Give some thought to the possi-bilities for unusual photographs—perhaps special effects—that will make the feature stand out. Very unconventional pictures, however, may have limited commercial value.

Shooting

Every picture should tell a story, but also fit into the planned series to enhance the whole. The photographs must have visual impact and variety, pace and cohesion. Some pictures should be quieter than others to vary the pace, and the camera technique should be changed to include the odd close-up or unexpected view. Take many variations of particular pictures to provide alterna-tives to choose from. Take portraits of individuals who are important. Work within the known limitations of your equipment—it is easy to get carried away and attempt the impossible, with predictable results. Other common mistakes in-clude the production of a collection of photo-graphs that do not form a natural series, having no coherent point, and a series which seems to consist of the same picture, in that lots of different people are shown doing the same thing. If the pictures are static, boring or repetitive the feature will not be a success.

The Imps

To illustrate the way in which a good feature be created, I chose the Imps Motorcycle Dis Team. The results appear on the previous page was an ideal subject. That a team of children young people between the ages of six and six should be capable of a daring and apparently gerous display of motorcycle acrobatics— formed to the highest professional standard was itself surprising. But the thing that impre me most was the way in which a bunch of End kids who would otherwise have found tructive outlets for their energy had become ciplined and committed, channelling their ene in such a positive way. This served as the basi the text—while the spectacular nature of display provided ample scope for a series exciting photographs.

Despite the widespread publicity received the Imps, nobody had thought of doing a pho feature. I visited the team, watched their p gramme, discussed it with them and planned series of photographs I wished to take. Wea conditions were far from perfect. Shooting t place on two separate days and I took as m variations on my chosen themes as possible provide sufficient pictures of usable quality to give a reasonable range of choice. The directors of magazines and newspapers tenc look through the full selection—and immedia ask for the one picture that isn't there.

With the full cooperation of the team—v were prepared to repeat stunts until I was satis —I eventually obtained all the material I wan The feature was instantly used by a natio newspaper.

Behind the glamour of display riding, there hours spent acquiring a sound knowledge of ho a motorbike works and maintaining equipment in immaculate condition.

The daredevil
IMPS

Excitement and dang
characterize the Imps
in action—yet six yea
of displays have pro-
duced only one injury
requiring hospital
treatment. Superb dis
cipline and months of
dedicated training—
channelling energies
that might otherwise
find a destructive out
let—go into this spec
tacular but safe displa
It makes the ideal su
ject for a series of
photographs with
visual drama and a
story to tell.

Index

Numbers in bold type refer to main entries in the book.

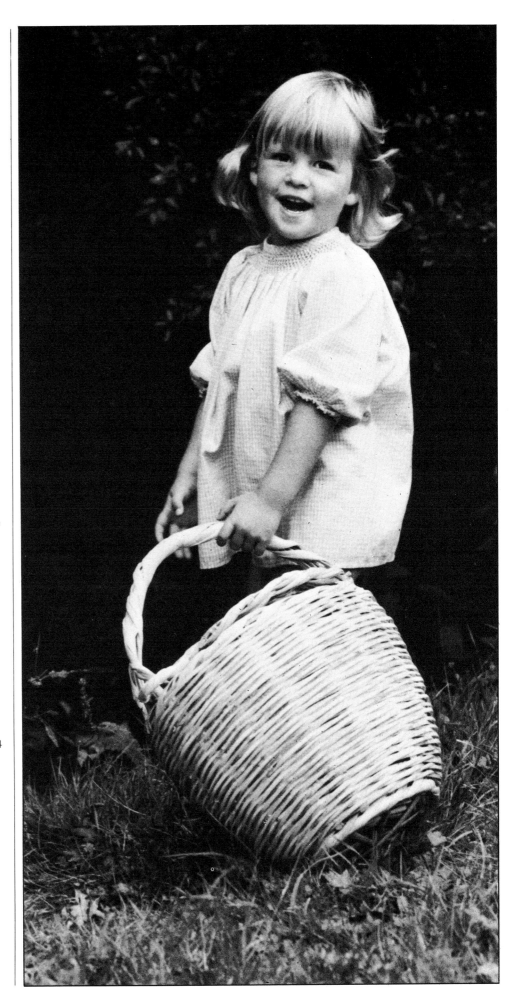

Acknowledgements

Art editor
Mel Petersen

Design assistant
Nigel O'Gorman

Technical consultant
Allan Shriver
Technical Editor
Amateur Photographer

Organizational researcher
Paddy Poynder

The author and publishers wish to thank the following people and
organizations for their help in preparing this book:
Julia Hedgecoe, Kate Duffy, Toby Hogarth, Robbie Hunter of the G. & S.
Skateboard Team, Tessa Marsh, Caroline Mazur, Roy Pratt and the Imps
Motorcycle Display Team

ARTISTS: Harry Clow, Tony Graham, Kevin Maddison, Andrew
Popkiewiez

RETOUCHER: Roy Flooks, O'Connor/Dowse

Italian Tourist Board, Jorge and Joe Koechlin Von Stein, Moroccan Tourist
Board, Olympus Optical Co (UK) Ltd, Pentax (UK) Ltd, Polaroid (UK)
Ltd, Portuguese Tourist Board, Vivitar (UK) Ltd